THE IMITATION OF CHRIST

Book I

A'KEMPIS THOMAS 1380-1471
TIMOTHY E. MOORE, ESQ.

Be an Imitator of Christ!

Tim Moore

CONTENTS

Opening Prayer to the Holy Spirit	v
Acknowledgments	ix
Foreword	xi
Why Read The Imitation of Christ?	xv
Who Should Read The Imitation of Christ?	xix
Life of Thomas a'Kempis	xxiii
The Chronicles of the Novice Master of Mount Saint Agnes Monastery.	xxvii
1. Introduction to the Fictional Narrative	1
2. Michaelmas, Anno Domini 1417	4
3. Mount Saint Agnes Monastery, Zwolle	10
4. The Imitation of Christ, by Thomas a'Kempis.	17
5. Having a Humble Opinion of Yourself	20
6. The Knowledge of Truth	23
7. Applying Prudence to Our Actions	27
8. Reading the Holy Scriptures	29
9. Inordinate Affections	31
10. Avoiding Vain Hope and Pride	33
11. The Dangers of Familiarity	35
12. Obedience and Subjection	37
13. Avoiding a Superfluity of Words	39
14. Acquiring Peace and Zeal for Our Spiritual Progress.	41
15. The Utility of Adversity	44
16. Resisting Temptations	46
17. Avoiding Rash Judgment	50
18. Works of Charity	52
19. Bearing the Faults of Others	54
20. The Consecrated Disciple	56
21. The Example of the Holy Fathers	58
22. The Spiritual Exercise of the Devout Disciple	61
23. The Love of Solitude and Silence	65

24. Compunction of Heart	69
25. Contemplation of the Miseries and Sorrows of This Life.	73
26. A Meditation Upon Death	78
27. The Judgment and Punishment of Sin	82
28. The Zealous Amendment of Our Whole Life.	86
29. Book II: Admonitions Concerning Interior Things.	91
About the Author	97
Appendix	99
Key Questions from Book I of The Imitation of Christ.	101
Key Quotes	105
Prayers	109

OPENING PRAYER TO THE HOLY SPIRIT

Come, Holy Spirit

Come, Holy Spirit, fill the hearts of the faithful: and enkindle in them the fire of Your love.
V. Send forth Your Spirit and they shall be created.
R. And You shall renew the face of the earth.
Let us pray. O God, Who instructed the hearts of the faithful by the light of the Holy Spirit, grant us in the same Spirit to be truly wise, and ever to rejoice in His consolation.
Through Christ our Lord. Amen.

DEDICATION

For my lovely wife, Donna, and our children (Cordelia, Virginia, Jim, Joe, Josh, Maria, John Paul, and your spouses and children, both those present and those yet to come!):
I love you and keep you always in my prayers.

ACKNOWLEDGMENTS

THANK YOU to all those who have encouraged me along the way - especially my family.

A special shout out to Miss Lila Martin, who told me to write this book about 8 years ago. Lila was my grade school math teacher, and opened new vistas of God's grace in my life through her teaching and prayerful example.

And in memory of my Dad, Jim Moore, who introduced me to The Imitation and set an example for me. Thanks, Dad. By God's Grace, I'll see you in Heaven. And thank you to my Mom, Rose, who continually inspires me.

Thank you to my beta readers for your suggestions, edits, and candid remarks.

Thank you to the Church of the Blessed Sacrament and its 24 hour Adoration Chapel, at which most of this manuscript was poured over, edited, prayed over, and, at one time, completely deleted! This work was composed under our Lord's watch - week after week. I offer it up for His glory and His Blessing, through the intercession of Thomas a'Kempis.

FOREWORD

When I was a boy, as part of my chores, I used to go into my parents room to vacuum and dust. Upon one such occasion, I came across a tattered, pocket-sized edition of a book titled, "The Imitation of Christ." My father, Jim, was not a big reader, but he had read this and read it to the point that the cover became well-worn.

This ignited a curiosity in me, since my Dad was a minimalist when it came to prayer-books devotionals. In talking with Dad, he indicated that the words spoken to him in a more real sense than other books. So, in imitating my Dad, I picked up a copy, and since then my love of this book has grown and blossomed.

Over the years, I've studied *The Imitation*. The book and its writer, Thomas a'Kempis, have prodded me to go deeper in my relationship with my Lord Jesus Christ. I am regularly challenged to strip the vanity and sin from my life: not from a sense of obligation, chastisement or performance-based theology, but rather because of my Love for Jesus Christ.

When my Dad died, I received his copy of *The Imitation*. I have it still, and it's more well-worn than ever, because I need to meditate on its teachings more than ever. Super-glue works great on books that defy re-covering.

FOREWORD

Over the years, I've collected many copies of *The Imitation*. My favorites, like Dad's, are all in an older English translation, with many "saiths" and "thous" and "hasts". This version attempts to update the language into a more readable form without dumbing down the underlying content. No mean task in the 21st Century. Along the way, I consulted many fine editions of *The Imitation*, to try and get it just right.

My hope is that you will find and experience the same depth of devotion and love of Christ, which Thomas brings to us so well. At times, you will want to put yourself in a monk's habit and sit at the Master's feet (Rm 10:15). At other times, you will bring your burdens to this book and find that all your worries are your own vanity: that in the scheme of things, weighed against our immortal soul and the eternal relationship with God, those burdens are nothing – a chasing after the wind (Eccl 1:14). In future volumes, Christ Himself will emerge from the pages to counsel and encourage us, and admonish us to follow Him at all times, in all situations. He will do so with compassion and love, but with an unwavering sense of courage. When Rome is burning, He will appear as we are running away and ask us: "Quo Vadis?" Where are you going?

In reading and researching the life of Thomas a'Kempis, I have come to the conclusion that Thomas had visions of Christ doing the work that Thomas himself was actually doing. Some of his writings and other writings about him suggest that to be the case.

Here was a man so in tune with the Spirit, so focused on the mission of the Gospel that he regularly encountered Christ in this way. In Thomas' eyes, it was Christ Himself, physically present, doing the charitable work – with Thomas a mere observer. This is why I included a fictional narrative at the beginning of Book 1 (and those to follow). My hope is to share the mind of Thomas with you as he may have seen himself as the chronicler of Mount St. Agnes Monastery.

In our age, it would be as if Thomas were wearing a GoPro Camera, but the lens was showing to Thomas the Hands of Christ, the Feet of Christ, the whole Person of Christ performing the good work or charitable deed. During a time of famine, for example, Thomas comes into the priory during meal time and tells the monks that they must divide their meager share of bread in half in order to feed the starving people of the village. And they did.

I believe that Thomas a'Kempis, as a mystic, heard the words of Christ during instances like this (and there were many). Those around him did not question his inspiration. It was as if he were simply following directions, taking notes, showing up. May we do likewise by stripping the distractions and sin from our lives so that we may imitate Thomas and hear the Voice of Christ.

Tim Moore, Springfield Illinois, Feast of Thomas a'Kempis, July 25th, 2017.

WHY READ THE IMITATION OF CHRIST?

This book is best taken in short doses. That is, I recommend that you read one chapter a day. You may want to work through a whole book or just take random chapters, but taking one chapter at a time and meditating on that chapter is the best way to work through The Imitation of Christ (*The Imitation*).

There are times when you will hit upon a verse in a chapter that is profound or moving or just makes you think. If this happens, then stop, take the time to ponder the verse, and then move on. Your reward will be a fruitful, spiritual progression toward following Christ.

For example, recently I was going through a certain meditation and the time, place and context of the meditation-as-prayer brought me to a tearful moment of thanks to Almighty God for His super-abundance. Of course I had read that passage many times, over many years. But that day, at that moment, it struck me in that inspiring way.

To that purpose, there is no "end" to *The Imitation*. You don't "finish" it any more than you finish reading the Psalms, Gospels, or any timeless prayer. There are some passages you may want to turn to regularly because the wisdom and piety are so deep that I know Thomas and The Lord will quickly transport you to a place of holy perspective. Remember to open your reading with prayer. Ask the Holy Spirit to

WHY READ THE IMITATION OF CHRIST?

awaken His Spirit within your reading. I've put a prayer to the Holy Spirit in the front of the book for you to make it easy. You don't have to use this one, it's simply my favorite. Sometimes, when I forget to say this prayer, I just say: "Holy Spirit, please guide my prayerful reading today. May I bear fruit for You." At this invitation, the Holy Spirit will shed light upon even the tiniest portions of this book. After all, it's His book. Once you've prayed and selected your passage, don't rush through the chapter. Slow is good. Be methodical. Chew on the concepts and the words. Many verses have references to Holy Scripture. Check those out as well. Indeed, you might take a verse such as this from Chapter 11: "If every year we rooted out one vice, we would soon become perfect." You may meditate on those ideas all day, write these on your white board or a sticky note. You may find yourself still thinking of this concept a week later.

Many wonderful, soulful prayers appear in *The Imitation*, but only two in the first book at Chapters 3 and 19. In the other books, sometimes the entire chapter can be a prayer. However, where Thomas has offset the text specifically as a prayer, I've italicized that portion of the text. For example, prayers such as this one appear in Book 1, Chapter 3, The Knowledge of Truth:

> O God, You who are the Truth,
> make me one with You in everlasting love.
> It often wearies me to read and listen to many things.
> All that I wish for and desire is in You.
> Let all the doctors hold their peace;
> Let all creation keep silence before You.
> Speak alone to me, Lord.
> Amen.

Accordingly, in each book, these identified prayers and other similar prayerful interludes, are listed in the Appendix. You can turn to these to pray when that particular subject matter is presenting itself, or pray these on their own, since many are straight praise or worship. Or, you will find many spontaneous textual prayers of praise and plea and thanksgiving, such as the words in Book 4, Chapter 9, where the whole

Chapter is really a prayer...I promise I won't italicize the full chapter! I'll make some other notation. Finally, not everything that is a prayer is necessarily identified, since, as mentioned above, *The Imitation* can be mined again and again. Recently a friend suggested that I pair up certain meditations for the Rosary, like I am planning in Book II with the Stations of the Cross. Perhaps in Book III or IV or on my website (timothyedmoore.com).

In the Appendix, the Key Questions and Key Quotes from each chapter are listed for your convenience and reflection.

WHO SHOULD READ THE IMITATION OF CHRIST?

Any person who is interested in developing a walk with Christ should read this book. This Book is the second most widely read book in Christendom, the Holy Bible being first. There is guidance and counsel and wisdom for the holiest saint and the most depraved sinner.

For the new Christian, *The Imitation* will gently guide them into the life of a disciple. For the mature Christian, there is a deep understanding of the faith that Thomas brings to the pages that will challenge anyone's daily walk, even Popes (It is reported that Pope John Paul I, upon his death, was discovered to have had a copy of The Imitation at his bedside.).

Non-believers should read it to see the depths of peace offered by The Christ, for its insights into the human condition, and for general wisdom. People of other faith-walks should read it to discover and understand the prayerful nature and manner of devout Christians. Or for insight into Christ's Passion.

So, the answer is: Everyone who is seeking answers to living a life of holiness or pursuing time tested wisdom should read The Imitation of Christ.

The Imitation of Christ has been divided into four books. This is Book One. It isn't generally known which one was composed first.

WHO SHOULD READ THE IMITATION OF CHRIST?

However, the natural order of the books is based upon the historical view that the first book was written for an audience of novices entering the monastery at Mount St. Agnes, just outside of Zwolle, Netherlands. So its purpose is to help the novice shed his worldly affections and trappings, exchanging these for holiness and obedience.

The Second Book, on developing the interior life, presupposes a disciple that has been through this purgative stage of the new novice. The disciple is now inwardly focused, learning that "The Kingdom of God is within You."

Book Two takes measures to help the disciple face the vices and faults that we keep hidden in the recesses of our heart and mind. Thomas introduces the disciple to the burden of the sin which is borne by Christ: and comes face-to-face with Christ's command to "Take up your Cross and follow Me."

The Third Book develops the mature believer through personal conversations with Christ. Jesus enters the cell of His follower and asks questions, delivers admonitions, renders grace, offers words of comfort. The Third Book is the longest. It explores new ground in old territory, digs deeper into the roots of whatever is holding back His follower. Many topics explored there are meant to prod the disciple out of his stupor.

The Fourth Book is devoted to The Blessed Sacrament - The true Presence of Christ in the consecrated Eucharistic Host. It is a tenant of the Christian faith that earthly intimacy with Christ is obtained by consuming the Body of Christ, where our Lord condescends to be with us as Holy Bread. The Fourth Book is devoted to this ancient, Christ-commanded form of worship. Like the Holy Trinity, our love is enhanced within a community. And the shared community is sanctified by the sharing of The Body and Blood of Christ. While some chapters are oriented specifically toward the priest, any believer may benefit, as we are all part of the priesthood of the people.

It is my plan to treat each book separately. I have included Chapter 1 of Book II at the end of the text of Book I in order to give you a sample of it. Each book will have similar commentaries and a fictional narrative.

WHO SHOULD READ THE IMITATION OF CHRIST?

LIFE OF THOMAS A'KEMPIS

Thomas a'Kempis, nee Thomas Haemerken ("little hammer"), was born in Kempen, Germany, around 1380. His father, John, was a blacksmith by trade, but more likely a silversmith. Gertrude, his mother, was a school teacher. His brother, John, or Jan, was also a monk and became a prior of the abbey of Mount St Agnes. Jan joined the Brethren of the Common Life at Deventer and Windesheim a dozen years before Thomas.

Thomas a'Kempis

In 1392 Thomas followed Jan to Deventer in order to attend the

Latin school under Prior Florentius Radewyns, one of the founders of the Brethren of the Common Life. The Brethren were started by Gerard Groote and the Modern Devotion. Prior Radewyns was Groote's right hand man and successor.

This community took no vows, but lived a life which was meant to be an example to not only the clergy, but to the lay population. The Modern Devotion's community was therefore not strictly tied to the clergy, but yet took on the disciplines of poverty, chastity and obedience. Thomas attended the Latin school in Deventer from 1392 to 1399 and was heavily influenced by the Devout Brothers and Sisters.

After leaving school, Thomas traveled to Zwolle to visit his brother. Jan had become the prior of the new monastery at Mount St. Agnes, just outside of Zwolle, after a short stint at Windesheim. Thereafter, Thomas became a monk at Mount St. Agnes in 1406, becoming an ordained priest in 1413.

During his life there, Thomas held several positions in the monastery, including Novice Master and Sub-prior. Thomas and his brothers became prolific copyists since the monastery raised money through copying books and creating devotionals. The small books which fit into a leather purse were popular at the time and considered fashionable as these were worn about the belt and showed that the wearer was a person of some learning.

As sub-prior, he was also the Novice Master: his main role was to instruct novices - the newly admitted to the monastery. It was during this time that The Imitation began to take shape. Mt. Saint Agnes was a quiet place, but Thomas and his Brothers interacted readily with the communities around them. Leading a quiet life, outside of his role as priest, the majority of his time was spent in writing, instructing his novices, and reading.

The monastery underwent an interdict in 1429. This meant that Christian services were suspended and the administration of sacraments, except for baptism, confession, and last rites, were halted. Even Mass was prohibited and the dead were denied Christian burial. The pope of the time, Pope Martin V, had rejected the bishop-elect of Utrecht, as a political affront to him. So, in obedience, the monks left Mt. St. Agnes for two years. During that time, Thomas traveled to Arnhem, in the eastern part of the Netherlands, to care for Jan, who was dying, and remained there until Jan died in 1432.

We know that Thomas copied the Bible at least four times: With some books, probably multiple times because certain books were more popular than others; e.g., Exodus over Leviticus.

The Imitation has direct quotes from or allusions to Scripture at every turn of the page. I have cited many along the way, but did not track them all for fear of overwhelming you. At one scholar's count, there are over 8,000 Scriptural allusions in the The Imitation (when counting all four books).

Thomas has been described as a man of average height to short, with a dark complexion and sharp features, a broad forehead and piercing eyes. He was affable and gentle but not given to small talk. He loved to preach about The Passion of our Lord. When asked about matters of passing importance, he was purported to have said: "My brothers, I must go: Someone is waiting to converse with me in my cell."

Likewise, his great past time was reading. One famous portrait of him bears as his motto: "Everywhere I have sought rest and found it no where, save in little nooks with little books."

The original text was rendered in Latin, in verse format. The English versions of this format are quite beautiful. However, for ease of reading, I've kept the text to prose, but tried to stay true to the rhythm of the words.

Some scholars dispute as to who actually wrote The Imitation, but Thomas is generally credited with the work. That said, as Thomas was well-read and studied in the texts of his masters (Groote, Radewyns, and others), it is likely that the Imitation is an amalgam or synthesis of many devotional writings.

Thomas did claim authorship, albeit in a humble way, in that in one edition of the Imitation he signed the work. His humility was such that he would be aghast at the notion of fame being attached to his name, let alone for a work that he did for the glory of God and God's disciples. My guess is that his signature was simply a fact chronicled by him as completing the work.

Good Thomas died in 1471 near Zwolle, Netherlands. It is said that he was buried alive, and thus is not a canonized Saint of the Catholic Church. For more on this, see my blog entry entitled: "Why Isn't Thomas a'Kempis a Saint of the Catholic Church?" at timothyedmoore.com. For me, the man is a saint, which simply means that he led a life worthy of emulation (or imitation). His Feast Day is generally reckoned as July 25th which is the Feast of St. James the Less.

Thomas was originally buried in the cemetery of Mt. St. Agnes. Over the years, his remains were moved from one location to another. When my wife, Donna, and I visited Zwolle in 2014, His reliquary was entombed at the Church of the Assumption.

THE CHRONICLES OF THE NOVICE MASTER OF MOUNT SAINT AGNES MONASTERY.

A FICTIONAL NARRATIVE ON THE WRITING OF BOOK ONE OF THE IMITATION OF CHRIST, BY TIMOTHY E. MOORE

**Mount Saint Agnes Monastery, Zwolle.
Feast of St. Michael**

Tunic of Thomas a'Kempis

I

INTRODUCTION TO THE FICTIONAL NARRATIVE

In developing these themes, and reading many (if not all) of the writings of Thomas a'Kempis, and many writings about him, I have taken the liberty of writing a fictional narrative from the point of view of Thomas.

This narrative is an attempt to get into the mind of Thomas and provide you with his perspective as the Novice Master of the Mount Saint Agnes Monastery, and why he composed these books. These are my own suppositions and notions. The narratives are meant to bring you to a place and time in the early 15th Century, and immerse you into the realm of this holy monk, his peers and his novices (of which I am one).

The setting of late medieval Europe is a world much like our own times – there is much chaos and war. People are divided and fed up with this system or that. The marginalized are ignored and left to consume themselves in their poverty. The Hundred Years War or its vestiges caused great turbulence throughout that part of the world, especially among the common people who were simply pawns of the remnants of the feudal system.

In the Netherlands, the country was not a country, but a set of provinces under the control of Spain, with a great deal of influence of France and Germany. The Netherlands were on the periphery of the wars and battles. But their burden was the growing wealth of the Dutch, which attracted the attention of the royalty of the time, who always needed more taxes to fund their wars, and turned to the Low Countries to fund these wars. And then there was the Black Death.

The Plague had hit hardest in 1348. It shook the foundations of all the institutions of the time, since none were immune to its devastation. It is reported that up to one third of Europe's population were wiped out in a two year period. Thomas' parents were living through this, and it certainly affected how they lived their lives, and may explain why young Thomas was sent to the Latin School at Deventer at such a young age.

The Black Death impacted the culture and lead to significant questioning of the moorings of society. This included a severe shaking of the feudal systems and, coupled with the rising merchant class, reorganized the division of labor – since there was a shortage of people to work the land. The plague impacted the world Thomas' generation inherited in many bizarre ways: from rampant, fatalistic immorality upon the announcement of the plague spreading through a region, to mass (and extreme) penitence in hopes of placating an angry God, to bizarre medical concepts in hopes of finding a cure or treating the dread disease.

While the major outbreak had run its course by Thomas' time, the plague would break out from time to time, without warning. Thomas talks of it frequently in his Chronicles. In one writing, it alludes to the notion that Thomas may have survived an outbreak of the Black Death. Such people were seen as being anointed by God. And certainly Thomas was. Accordingly, the fictional narrative tries to include these concepts, trends and societal structures without overwhelming the reader.

The story begins with the death of Thomas' mentor and friend, Father Finn Van Zwarte, who was the Novice Master – a very important role in the monastery. The Novice Master is the Sub-Prior, that is, second in charge of the monastery. The Prior, Jan a'Kempis, is Thomas' older brother by at least twelve years.

Once the new Novice Master is named, he sets out to explain his mission and goals for his charges, the novices. This challenge puts him in the mind of writing a spiritual guidebook. I hope you enjoy these interludes. These narratives will continue in Books II, III, and IV.

Tim Moore, Feast of St. Augustine of Hippo, 2017.

2

MICHAELMAS, ANNO DOMINI 1417

"Lord, You brought my soul up from Sheol;
You let me live, from going down to the pit."

Psalm 30:4

IN THAT SAME YEAR, the following events are recalled on the Eve of St. Michael's, beginning with the sudden discovery of the body of our holy Brother and teacher, Father Finn Van Zwarte, the Novice Master. His lifeless body was found in his cell at Vigils, bed side in a kneeling position, as if in a plea for mercy. It is our guess that he had been dead since just after Compline, as his limbs had begun to stiffen. It is our guess that the novice assigned to awaken him was fooled into thinking that Fr. Van Zwarte had simply been in prayer. It is our guess that the novice was fearful of disturbing the priest.

The monastery is in deep mourning over this sudden passing. Friend to many, counselor to few. He imitated our Lord in most every way imaginable. His following of Christ was the greatest teaching example to the novices.

Fr. Van Zwarte was eulogized as a beloved mentor. As a Brother, Priest and former Dean, he came to understand his vocation late into his priesthood after having a radical conversion at the hands of our Lord. From that point on, he gained a deserved reputation for holiness and preaching, and his devotion to the development of the novices. Perhaps someday, future generations will celebrate this day as the Feast of St. Finn Van Zwarte.

But that is a tale for another time and another place, and another Feast Day. For now, we must be content with his passing on Michaelmas Eve for "He is risen, therefore he can be laid in the grave." This has great meaning for it portends that Fr. Van Zwarte's soul has found the risen Christ, and therefore he will be safe in death as we lay him in the grave with this confidence.

We buried him in the new cemetery to the south of the Chapel, next to Brother Wolford, as these two had been of the four original Brothers here (that is, The Brethren of the Common Life of the New Devotion, as founded by our venerable father, Gerard Groote).

The Brothers were then assembled by Prior Johan Haemerken, that is, Jan a'Kempis, at Mount St. Agnes and prayed earnestly for guidance to the Saints. Prior Jan invoked the Holy Spirit during his exhortation to the community: the immediate need of a Novice Master to replace Father Van Zwarte.

Prior Jan paced the Chapel. He looked into the eyes of each senior priest as he sought God's guidance as to which would fill the role. None met his eye. Most looked away either in humility, or simple avoidance. The role of Novice Master is a demanding one and under constant scrutiny. The Novice Master is required to be familiar with worldlings. A glib attitude is part of the charism needed to manage the many temptations which arise out of that life. The Novice Master must set the example for the novices and the congregation at all times.

His opportunity to sin and be exposed to depraved demeanors and temptations is greater than that of any other Brother, except, perhaps, the Prior himself. After all, the Brothers chose to separate themselves from such a life.

Prior Jan continued his exhortation with his mighty voice, his long form animating his spastic words and pleas. He often turned toward the Tabernacle, wringing his hands and pulling at the edges of his tonsured hair in pleading. He laid himself prostrate on the cold dirt floor, stretching out his arms as if on the Cross...followed by silence. The Brethren did likewise and prostrated themselves in mortification. Prior Jan could easily command one of them to the position, but that was not his way. He wanted - demanded even - that the selection should come from God. The floor warmed with the bodies spread upon it. Had some stranger entered, he'd have suspected an attack of Brigands had taken place. The men laid there, motionless, until midday prayer. Since Prior Jan had declared a fast for the intercession of the Holy Spirit, no food was taken. The Brethren remained in the Chapel, foregoing lunch and then supper as the day wore on.

No sound was heard save the breathing of the monks and the chatter of the birds. The silence was interrupted only by prayer at Vespers. The song that filled the rafters of the Chapel was absorbed into the spirits of the brethren, giving them strength of purpose.

No light displaced the encroaching darkness, save the lonely candle at the Tabernacle whose wick struggled to stay lit. As the moonless night progressed, the Brethren remained in silent prayer, taking a little sleep by way of standing or walking in procession around the interior of the Chapel. At three, they began Vigils and gathered again for Lauds at six, followed by Holy Mass.

During Holy Mass, Prior Jan and those senior priests concelebrating with him prayed a Mass of Repentance and Mourning, wearing their black vestments even though it was now the Feast of St. Michael, the patron of the Zwolle Deanery. The congregation felt the effects of the extended fast and night long vigil, receiving the Bread of Life with aching hunger.

Normally, following Mass, the Brethren would assemble for a morning meal of groats and seasonal fruit. Normally, on a Feast such as this, the Brethren may be treated to some eggs or fancy bread in celebration of the Holy Day.

NOT SO THIS DAY. THE BRETHREN ARRIVED AT THE REFECTORY HALL and were greeted by bare tables.

Brother Bakker, Master of the Larder, had also been in prayer the whole night and therefore no food had been prepared. He exited the larder with two meager loaves of stale bread from the previous day. He had intended to add the bread to a soup for the mid-day meal. Now it was hard and difficult on the tooth. Prior Jan held out his hands to receive the bread and Brother Bakker placed the loaves into the Prior's hands in a bow of offering. The Prior blessed the bread and elevated the two pieces for all to see. The Brothers raised their hands in unison toward the Prior to joining the communal blessing. Taking none for himself, he offered thanks and then with a whisper passed half of the loaf to Brother Bakker and the other half to Brother Dismas who did likewise.

The bread was passed on one side, first to the Novices. And on the other side, to the priests, starting with those recently ordained.

The Bread traveled from one man to the next, each taking a pinch or a lump or a crust as it made its way to the more senior men. As the shrinking loaf was passed along, Prior Jan watched with prayerful interest as each member took his share. Some ate their share immediately, others waited for some remark or nod of permission from the Prior, who, with eye contact, assented.

When it reached the last row of the priests, the half-loaf was now down to a quarter. It was obvious that there would not be enough for each man to have a portion if everyone took a like-sized share. Nevertheless, the men took and took and took, with still twelve men to feed.

The loaf arrived at the seventh priest, who received the loaf and, holding it like a whelping baby, began to weep quietly, looking at the bread as if it were a hungry child. He looked at his brother, the Prior, and, without remark, passed it to his fellow priest, Fr. Emmet DeVries. Puzzled, Fr. DeVries took a share and passed it. On it went to each man. Some took smaller portions, with that sacrifice made up by the gluttony of the next recipient. The loaf was now crumbling and the final two men took the small portion and divided it between them.

The bread now consumed, the Prior chanted this verse to his sheep:

> *"For His anger lasts but a moment;*
> *His favor a lifetime."*

And they chanted back to him.

> *"At dusk weeping comes for the night;*
> *But at dawn there is rejoicing."*
> Psalm 30:6

PRIOR JAN STOOD, LAUGHING; AN UNUSUAL OUTBURST CONSIDERING the solemn nature of this situation. Furthermore, laughter was considered a vanity and a mark of worldliness among the Brethren. He laughed aloud. To the surprise of the congregation, the Prior leaped and jumped and hooted with laughter. The Brothers, looking about at each other, began to giggle and laugh at his antics. Prior Jan burst out with a song of joy as he danced about the refectory, praising God. Like King David, he moved with wild abandon, stopping with outstretched arms in front of the ever-present creche. He lifted the statue of the Child Jesus, and began to march about the room, calling his Brothers to follow him outside the refectory. The confused Brothers joining in with fits and starts, rose and marched. Soon, all the Brothers were singing and smiling and raising their hands in praise, their faces upturned to God's gaze and blessing.

⚜

THE LANKY PRIOR LED HIS MEN IN A TRIUMPHAL MARCH AROUND the Chapel. Seven times they circled the holy building. At the seventh, they entered the Chapel and processed up the center of the church in quiet order, as they did by reverent habit. The men took their places in the stalls as the young Prior paced back and forth with the statue of the Christ Child. He wept quietly and without notice, save one.

He chanted to them again:

"You changed my mourning into dancing;"
    And they responded.
    "You took off my sackcloth and clothed me with gladness."

And then they all sang out together:

> *"So that my glory may praise You, and not be silent.*
> *O Lord, my God, forever will I give You thanks."*
> *Psalm 30:12-13*

Prior Jan called out in prayer, lifting the statue of the Child toward the Tabernacle in praise and thanksgiving. He then turned and walked toward the congregants. All eyes followed him as he moved toward the stall of priests. Carrying the statue as if it were alive, patting it and holding it in the crook of his left arm, the tall Prior raised his long right arm out over the priests, closing his eyes and praying quietly. He stopped in front of the seventh man, the diminutive priest who had forsaken his share of bread so that the others might be fed. Prior Jan took the Child from his care and placed it with reverential gentleness into the arms of the smaller man. With long, tear filled eyes, the young priest accepted the Child, kissing its forehead and offering it back to his brother, and the Prior with glad tears, motioned refusal. The younger priest cradled the Child Jesus and, bowing his head over the statue, began to sob. The Prior laid his hands on the head of his younger brother Thomas (of Kempen) and with a loud voice, prayed the prayer of installation, declaring this man to be the new Novice Master.

3
MOUNT SAINT AGNES MONASTERY, ZWOLLE

FEAST OF ST. NICHOLAS

IN THAT SAME YEAR, in obedience to Prior Jan, and as Novice Master, this writing is meant to chronicle the plans, admonitions, considerations, and plans for the direction of our novices.

Mainly, it documents the methods employed in taking the new acolyte through the purgative process- transitioning them from their world into the world of the Monastery at Mount St. Agnes.

Prior Jan's directive is also meant as a record for sharing these ideas with other monasteries as our order grows. So this short undertaking is for those who would seek to imitate our methods. Our meditation on the imitation of Christ is the fruit of this undertaking.

Since the days of the venerable Fr. Van Zwarte, the new Novice Master has gone to great lengths to not only chronicle the teachings and methods of Van Zwarte and his predecessors, but also create reflections for this community that may be used to deepen our prayer life or refresh our acquaintance with what the novice encounters upon entering our congregation.

It is a difficult task to instruct worldlings who feel called to the religious life. Some are not called at all, but turn to the monastery as a best bad choice. Likewise, some are brought to us through the popular curiosity that has arisen around the Modern Devotion as founded by our Father, Gerard Groote (Gerard Magnus). Others show up at our doorstep from necessity or from poverty - they are the unwanted. Still others arrive in carriages and on horses, the sons of privilege who are playing a waiting game. Not surprisingly, we see novices who come to make recompense for a life spent in sin, war, exploitation, and gluttony. These come to wash their very selves from the world - they seek peace.

They will come from their cities and farms, their castles and hovels, their forges and mills. While some will arrive on horses or by mule, most will simply walk. Whether by carriage, on foot, or by wagon, they will come with the dust of the world in every crevice of their body. Most will be from poverty - real poverty, seeking relief or "an easy road" of privilege and sustenance that they believe is the daily life of the clergy. Most believe the rumors of our detractors - that we are handed tithes and other privileges which entitle us to a life of ease. They will learn otherwise.

Those novices who are wealthy will arrive with an expectation of entitlement and an air of superiority. As second or third born sons whose inheritance is assured only by the death of their brothers, they too will perceive this to be an easy life where they can await the news of the death of their loved one. They will learn otherwise.

Perhaps they will wish they had joined the army. Perhaps they will wish they had stayed at the counting house. Perhaps they will learn to speak the language of love offered by the simple poverty of the Cross of our Lord.

Here, under the blessed example of Prior Jan, they will don the simple, patch laden frock of the novice alongside their poorer brothers. The tonsured haircuts they receive will look just as ridiculous on them as that of the peasant novice from the smithy. The mean food and drink will have them all, like the Israelites, dreaming of the leaks of Egypt.

And yet, Christ will call out to them to become "fishers of men." Somewhere along the Way of the novitiate, they will encounter The Christ. Jesus Himself will meet them. Many will respond to His call. Some will ignore His call. But the call will come.

Yes, God has other plans for them. Through His Holy Spirit, their days will be filled with productive labor that helps to feed the poor. Or they may be engaged as workers to build the monastery orchard, one of the dozens of minor tasks which engender humility. They will find that God's presence may be found in the close, mean quarters of nature. All laced with prayer, of course.

Like the late Brother Van Zwarte, they will take part in the common labors and lowly tasks such as washing the trenches, removing stones from the fields, gleaning sticks for the kitchen fire to make pulse. It was also his nature to come to the choir loft early to monitor his novices. And I will imitate him, both in labor and in supervision of my charges, so that these novices will learn that no one is above such tasks. That it is all for God's glory.

From Lauds to Compline we will weave their days and nights together with His presence, and praise Him without ceasing. We will teach them that when they are hungry, that the Lord Himself will be their Bread. We will slake their thirst with the sweat and blood of Christ. When they need to bathe, we will wash them in the Scriptures, Holy Mass and humble works of charity.

During the spring floods, we will join the farmers in the mud, draining the field to save the crop. When the villagers are starving, we will feed them our bread and our pulse- sharing in their hunger and poverty. These men will be examples of Christ at work. By standing in for Christ, by imitating Him, He will lead he novice to look forward to such opportunities.

At the beginning of their life here, when they are helping put up hay in the morning, they will only see the steam come off the hay. As they grow in their faith, the Lord will open their eyes. They will begin to see the rising steam as their prayer, like incense rising from their efforts to His glory. When that time comes, they will cry out: "You duped me, Lord, and I let myself be duped (Jer 20:7)!"

In the scriptorium, they will copy sacred texts. Their eyes will ache from straining at the pages and their fingers will ache from the constant motion of the feather quill. Their hands will be stained with the black blood of the ink. And just as their minds will begin to wander with the boredom of repetitive, careful scrivening, relief will come. Chores will rotate from the scribe to the butcher, laying aside the quill and picking up the scraping knife to put a keen edge on it-thus removing the bits of fat and hair from the vellum. Those binding the books will tear their knuckles on the raw wooden covers. As the binders hull the wood with the saw so they will be stripped of their bark and worn smooth. The brothers will learn to tie the finished leaves together to make a book of quality.

Their own sharp edges and hard headed selfishness will be gently worn away by the daily encounter with hard poverty. Their voices will grow hoarse with the constant begging of our Lord for mercy toward His people. At the end of their novitiate, when they choose to take the cowl, many of the hard edges and rough spots will be made smooth. Our Lord Himself will make straight their crookedness through His Own example.

And so, my prayer is to leave their conversion to Him. I will simply provide occasions and opportunities for these men, and step out of the way of the Spirit. I won't leave them or forsake them: it will be my duty to provide spiritual direction and guidance and to admonish these worldlings on The Way of our Lord. It will be my duty to instruct them and encourage them to choose one path over another - correct them on even the most minor of worldly conduct - gently, of course, and rescue them from themselves. It will be my duty to help them become followers of Christ.

Only Christ can reveal to each seeker what cross is prepared for him. His Way is narrow. His Way is clear. His Way is the Way of the Cross. It the role of the Novice Master to show them how to enter the narrow gate, and thereby how to embrace, journey, and imitate our Lord Jesus Christ. And so, I have laid down some precepts for the novices to study and meditate upon, as I and my predecessors have meditated and prayed on these maxims and collections. These "Useful Admonitions" are for their instruction in the Common Life. However, in reviewing these texts for copying in the scriptorium, I found myself refreshed anew at considering each admonition as applied, once again, to my own life.

Prior Jan discussed this notion with the other leaders of Mount St. Agnes and took it to prayer. Together, these admonitions were reviewed. The Brethren were then inspired to select those which moved us or which entries prompted us to recall our days as Novices.

And the result is here before you: We collected and recollected the ideas of the Modern Devotion laid down by our holy Founder, Gerard Groote, and expanded upon by my Master, the saintly Prior Florentius Radewyns.

My hope and prayer are that our novices will learn to shed their worldly ways through prayer and acts of charity, and self-denial. That they will enter into the monastic life with joy and humility that comes not from simply following Christ, but by imitating Him. Just as the great Saints of old - our Novices will grow in faith. Just as these Saints found Christ in the poor, we too will find Him in their eyes and hearts. During their journey toward holiness, they will encounter much adversity, little ease, and much discomfort. They will want consolation and find none. At times, they will want to give up... perhaps even to die. I want them to seek the Lord's will in these matters, and not look for miracles, only encounters with Christ.

If they will seek to imitate Christ, and not value the world's ideas; if they will pursue humility instead of the world's high opinion; if they will seek out the truth and exercise prudence as laid out in Holy Scripture, then they will start to become more Christ-like.

Their pitfalls lie with unhealthy carnal affections. The flesh is a good servant, but a poor master. Threats come from vanity and pride. Gossip and ill-discipline will prevent them from rising to new levels of perfection. If they can keep their familiarity in check, we can train them in obedience and in controlling their tongues. As they acquire zeal and peace in their spiritual journey, they will learn to study the great Saints.

We will teach them to prayerfully fast and abstain from more than food. This is in order to strengthen them against temptations. Fasting without prayer is simply starvation. Our novices will be reminded to pray as their hunger pains surge. Through bodily mortifications, we will redirect their passions away from the self, turning their mind to the sacrifice of the Cross.

The next challenge will be within the community itself. As our novices become part of the Brotherhood and shed their old ways, they will start to form new distasteful practices.

As they grow in sanctity, they will begin to seek out imperfections in others rather than in turning their critical eye upon themselves. But by performing works of charity, they will overcome this tendency - he who does much loves much.

In teaching them the practices of the monastic life, they will be grounded in subjecting themselves and their own wants to the betterment and peace of the community. In surveying the life of the Holy Fathers, the example will be pegged toward becoming soaked in the virtues needed by those in our holy community. By learning to love solitude and silence our novices will encounter God in their thoughts and quiet occupations, rather than through idle chatter and superfluous activities.

As the Lord reveals Himself to each novice, they will find progress through compunction of heart and thereby increase their devotion to Him. By turning to Him in troublesome times, and offering up their suffering for God's sake, they will unite their sufferings with those of our Lord. The novice must indeed die to himself, pursue and face just judgment of the worldly life, and seek to amend that old life with a new life in Christ.

Salvation is had by receiving Divine Life. We are not saved alone but in community. But in those alone moments, the novice will reflect upon imitating Christ, seeing our Lord as the model. Their room will become a sanctuary to reflect upon these grace-filled moments. But it will be in the community that their salvation will be most apparent. In the Mass, they will truly learn that visible things become the instruments of invisible grace. It is the community that will help the novice understand God's holy power revealed in the Blessed Sacrament,

Thus have I gazed upon you in the sanctuary to see Your power and Your glory, for Your kindness is a greater good than life; my lips shall glorify You.
Psalm 63:3-4

Our Father, St. Augustine liked to say that "you are what you love." Here we will teach the novice to love the community. We will teach the novice to love the self through the eyes of Christ, not the world. To empty himself of the traps and vain-glories and comforts and sores which the world has given him, and replace these with an interior life in Christ. One filled with humility, sacrifice, and salves - salves that relieve the pain of the world, as St. Paul says, by joining those sufferings with the Cross of Christ.

That is the Novice Master's plan. My concern is that in my zeal to bring these novices into the community, I will forget some key principle of monastic life or article of faith which may be the bridge from life in this world to life in the Spirit. It's unsettling, really, to assume this burden. These men will be my charges for quite some time, I feel responsible. I am responsible for seeing them through this part of their vocation. So, I will get out of the way and ask the Holy Spirit, the Paraclete, to fill the hearts of the faithful and enkindle in them (and me), the fire of His Love. Send forth Your Spirit, and we shall be created, and You shall renew the face of the earth. Amen.

❧ 4 ❦
THE IMITATION OF CHRIST, BY THOMAS A'KEMPIS.
USEFUL ADMONITIONS FOR THE SPIRITUAL LIFE.

EDITS AND COMMENTARY BY TIMOTHY E. MOORE

The Imitation of Christ, and of Contempt of the World and All Its Vanities.
   Chapter 1 Focus: We must know, love, serve and follow our Lord Jesus Christ. Knowing Christ's divinity is only one aspect book knowledge - whereas following Him in our daily lives is what it means to be one of His disciples. Thomas cautions us to understand the fleeting nature of the physical (carnal) world and its vanishing pleasures and empty accolades. Keeping our eyes upon Heaven will hold us in God's Grace.

This first chapter opens with an ominous statement and command:

"And then The Sign of the Cross Shall be in Heaven When the Lord Comes to Judge.
Deny Yourself, Take Up Your Cross, and Follow Me."

Thomas shocks us out of our world into turning our gaze toward Heaven.

The only sure path God has provided us is The Way of the Cross.

Question: What part of the Life of Christ will I meditate upon?

Chapter 1, In Short.

1. Dwelling upon the life of Jesus Christ is our most important task.
2. Conform your whole life to the mind of Christ.
3. A good life makes you dear to God.
4. It is vanity to seek after worldly honors and pleasures.
5. Stay in God's Grace by setting your heart upon the things of heaven.

THE TEXT ON USEFUL ADMONITIONS FOR THE SPIRITUAL LIFE: "AND THEN THE SIGN OF THE CROSS SHALL BE IN HEAVEN, WHEN THE LORD COMES TO JUDGE" (MT 24:30)."

> "Deny Yourself, Take Up Your Cross,
> and Follow Me."
> Matthew 16:24

"He that follows me shall not walk in darkness ," says the Lord."
John 12:12

These are the words of Christ. If we seek true illumination and deliverance from all blindness of heart His words teach us how far we must go to imitate His life and character. **Let it be our most earnest study, therefore, to dwell upon the life of Jesus Christ.**

2. Christ's teaching surpasses the teaching of all holy scholars, and as such those who have His Spirit find hidden manna (Rev 2:17). But there are many who, though they frequently hear the Gospel, feel little longing toward it. This is because they do not yet have the mind of Christ. If you, therefore, fully and with true wisdom understand the words of Christ, strive then to conform your whole life to the mind of Christ.

3. If you lack humility and thereby are displeasing to the Holy Trinity, what good is it for you to enter into deep discussions concerning

the Holy Trinity? For certainly it is not deep words that make you holy and upright, rather it is a good life which makes you dear to God. I would rather feel contrition than be skillful in its definition.

If you knew the whole Bible, and the sayings of all the philosophers, what would all this benefit you without the love and grace of God? Vanity of vanities, all life is vanity, save to love God and to serve only Him (Eccl 1:2). That is the highest wisdom, to cast the world behind us, and to reach forward to the heavenly kingdom.

4. It is vanity then to seek after, and to trust in, riches that shall perish. It is vanity, too, to covet honors and to lift up ourselves on high. It is vanity to follow the desires of the flesh and also be led by those desires. For in the end, this brings misery.

It is vanity to desire a long life and yet to have little care for a good life. It is vanity to only take thought for the life which now is being lived and not to look forward to the things which will be your reality in the hereafter. It is vanity to love that which quickly passes away and not to hasten where eternal joy abides.

5. Be mindful of the saying: "The eye is not satisfied with seeing, nor the ear with hearing (Eccl 1:8)." Strive, therefore, to turn away your heart from the love of things that are seen and instead set your heart upon those things that are not seen. For they who follow after their own fleshly desires defile the conscience and destroy the grace of God.

❧ 5 ☙
HAVING A HUMBLE OPINION OF YOURSELF

Chapter 2 Focus: Being humble requires perspective in that we compare ourselves constantly with others in our achievement, knowledge, and position. In modern slang, this is known as "comparisonitis." Thomas recognizes this natural tendency, advising us to view our lives from God's perspective. There's a point where we can obsess over the knowledge of a thing to our own detriment, and then, when it is time to employ that knowledge, we are useless because we may know about a thing but do nothing with that knowledge. Or that knowledge has little, if any, relevance to working out our salvation.

Thomas is hardly "anti-intellectual (See Chapter 3, for example.)" Rather, he tells us to face the truth that, ultimately, we cannot know everything. We should put our knowledge and skills towards a Godly purpose while deflecting excessive praise for our meager skills.

As an aside - "fear of the Lord" as used in this chapter and others simply means an awesome respect for God's power. It is like saying - "Be careful, child, the stove is hot!"

Questions: What does my life look like from God's perspective?

How am I using my knowledge and skills for God's Kingdom?

Chapter 2, In Short.

1. Your natural desire for knowledge is meaningless without fear of the Lord.

2. Refrain from all your excessive desires to know everything.

3. Be accountable for the knowledge given to you.

4. The most valuable lesson you can learn is this: To truly know and discount yourself.

THE TEXT ON HAVING A HUMBLE OPINION OF YOURSELF

Everyone naturally desires to know many things, but what does that knowledge do for you without a healthy fear and respect of God (Prov 9:10)? A simple peasant that serves God is better off than a proud scholar who watches the stars but neglects knowledge of himself (Sr 19:19-21).

Whoever knows himself well is of small worth in his own eyes and is embarrassed with being praised by others. If I knew all things in the world, but am not loving towards others, what does it profit me in God's sight? Who will judge me according to my deeds?

2. Refrain from your excessive desires to know all things, because what is found in that desire is only distraction and delusion. The learned desire to have the appearance of being wise and also of being called wise in the eyes of others. There are many things, the knowledge of which is of little or no value to your soul. You are foolish to pay any attention to the knowledge of things other than what serves your salvation. Many words do not satisfy the soul but a good life gives peace to the mind, and a pure conscience affords you great confidence in God.

3. The greater and more complete your knowledge the more severe will be your judgment unless your life is also more holy. Therefore do not be puffed up with any skill or knowledge, but rather be accountable for the knowledge which has been given to you.

If it seems to you that you know many things and understand many things well enough, know that at the same time there are many more things of which you know nothing at all. Do not be high-minded, but rather acknowledge your own ignorance. Why would you want to let yourself be above others when there are many others with more knowledge and skill in the Scriptures than you? If you would know and learn anything to its purpose, love to be unknown and be considered as nothing in the sight of others.

4. **The highest and most valuable lesson we can learn is this: To truly know and discount ourselves.** To have a low opinion of ourselves and to think always well and highly of others is great wisdom and high perfection. If you should see another person openly sin or commit some wicked crime you ought not to think of yourself as better than that person because you do not know how long you will remain in a good state of integrity and grace yourself. All of us are frail and weak but see that you do not think of anyone as more susceptible to sin than yourself.

6

THE KNOWLEDGE OF TRUTH

Chapter 3 Focus: Three Bible verses jump out at me when I prepared to read this chapter - All are from John's Gospel. The first occurs when Pilate asks our Lord: "What is truth (Jn 18:38)?" The second takes place in an earlier passage, where our Lord has the answer to Pilate's later question by answering: "I Am the Way, The Truth and The Life... (Jn 14:6)" and then finally - "The Truth will set you free (Jn 8:32)."

Pointing to these quotes will help as you meditate on this chapter. This is the only chapter in Book 1 with a full prayer. In that prayer, Thomas couples together Truth and Love. The remainder of the chapter examines our worldly feelings and judgments, and how that worldly lens distorts the Truth as Pilate did. The only filter to examine wisdom and knowledge and learning is God's Truth.

Thomas emphasizes that it is more important to practice the truths of the Faith than it is to understand the theology behind these truths. While we can enjoy the banquet of detailed thought behind God's plan for us, we must also live that life as He commands us. We must master our passions and live in holiness rather than chase after academic accolades. It is an unfortunate thing to know about eternal truths and salvific doctrines and then not put those into action. It is quite another to implement those truths in your life.

Question: How do I practice the truths of the Faith in my life?

Chapter 3, In Short.

1. Our own judgment and feelings often deceive us from the truth.
2. Without God, no one understands or rightly judges.
3. Our efforts should be spent in mastering ourselves.
4. A good conscience and a holy life are better than all learning.
5. On Judgment Day we will be asked if we have lived a holy life.
6. Having great charity is the only thing that makes you truly great.

THE TEXT ON THE KNOWLEDGE OF TRUTH

Happy are you whom Truth itself teaches, not by figures and transient words, but as it is in itself (Ps 94:12). Our own judgment and feelings often deceive us, and we discern very little of the truth. How does it profit you to argue about hidden and dark things, of which we know nothing, when we will not even be asked about such things during the Judgment? Oh, what serious folly it is to neglect the things which are beneficial and necessary and to give our minds to things which are curious and hurtful! Even having eyes, we do not see.

2. And why are we talking about genus and species! Whomever the Eternal Word addresses is free from multiple questioning. From this One Word are all things, and all things speak of Him; and this is the Beginning which also speaks to us (Nm 7:8).

Without God, no one understands or rightly judges. Those to whom all things are one, who brings all things to one, who sees all things in one, are able to remain steadfast in spirit, and at rest in God.

O God, You who are the Truth, make me one with You in everlasting love. It often wearies me to read and listen to many things. All that I wish for and desire is in You. Let all the doctors hold their peace; let all creation keep silence before You. Speak alone to me, Lord.

3. The more you have unity and simplicity in yourself, the more

easily these things come to you, and with a deeper understanding, because you receive the light of understanding from above. The pure, sincere, and steadfast spirit is not distracted by the many works to be done, because the spirit does all things to the honor of God, and strives to be free from all thoughts of self-seeking.

Who does more to hinder and annoy you more than your own undisciplined heart? A disciple who is good and devout arranges within the heart beforehand those works which must be done abroad. Such a one is not drawn away by the desires of an evil will but subjects everything to the judgment of right reason. Who has a harder battle to fight than those who strive for self-mastery? And this should be our endeavor, to master ourselves, and thus daily to grow stronger than our self, and go on to perfection.

4. All perfection has some imperfection joined to it in this life, and all our power of sight is not without some darkness. A lowly knowledge of yourself is a surer way to God than the deep searching of learning. Not that learning is to be blamed, nor the taking account of anything that is good, but a good conscience and a holy life are better than all learning. And because many seek knowledge rather than good living, they go astray and bear little or no fruit.

5. Oh, if they would give the same effort to the planting of virtues and rooting out vices which they now give to vain questionings, there would be fewer evil doings and stumbling-blocks among the laity, nor such lax living among houses of religion.

For certainly, on the Day of Judgment, it will be demanded of us, not what we have read but what we have done; not how well we have spoken, but whether we lived a holy life. Tell me now, where are all those masters and teachers, whom you knew so well while they were still with you and so accomplished in learning? Are not their teaching stalls now filled by others, who perhaps never have one thought concerning them? While they lived they seemed to be somewhat important, but now no one speaks of them.

6. Oh how quickly the glory of the world passes away! If only their life and knowledge had agreed together! For then they would have read and inquired to good purpose. How many perish through empty learning in this world, who care little for serving God. And because

they love to be great more than they love to be humble, they "have become vain in their imaginations (Rm 1:21)."

You are only truly great if you have great charity. You are only truly great if you deem yourself small and count the height of honor as nothing. You are only truly wise when you count all earthly things as dung so that you may win Christ. And the truly learned do the will of God and forsake their own will.

※ 7 ※
APPLYING PRUDENCE TO OUR ACTIONS

C**hapter 4 Focus**: Thomas has words of wisdom for us in our relationships with others. This is a practical chapter to follow up on the more esoteric chapters before. There are distinct applications here, and apt comparisons. Wagging tongues and rash actions are in direct opposition to loving kindness - regardless of the truth of the matter asserted or the perceived need of taking action. We will learn specific examples of this in Chapters 9 and 10 and 11. Meanwhile, don't spread the bad news, or listen to it. Rather, be prudent by spreading the Good News.

Prudence is tied closely to humility: balancing our decisions against what The Lord tells us in Scripture and Tradition. These decisions might seem rash until weighed against the Lord's perspective. Prudence should, therefore, come from our brain, lips, and hands as helping agents. This physical pragmatism flows from weighing the risks of carnality against a measured gain of positive, active outcomes which benefit the Mystical Body of Christ. Think of our Lord washing the feet of His disciples (John 13). To Peter, you, and me, this makes no sense. Peter (and we) speaks without thinking. But Christ clarifies everything as He shows us, and then tells us, how to lead with prudence.

Question: How am I prudent in my speech and actions?
Chapter 4, In Short.
1. Give time and attention to matters according to God's standard.
2. Do not to be rash in your actions or opinions.

THE TEXT ON APPLYING PRUDENCE TO OUR ACTIONS

We must be careful in giving credit to every word and suggestion by dedicating the necessary time and attention to weighing matters according to God's Standard.

Alas! We are so weak! We often readily believe and speak evil of others rather than good. But those seeking perfection do not easily give credit to every report because they know each other's weaknesses, which are prone to evil and always subject to a slip of the tongue.

2. There is great wisdom in not acting rashly in our daily business. Neither is it helpful to be hard-hearted in our opinions. We should not believe every report, nor in-the-moment tell others the things which we have heard or believed. Consult with someone who is wise and conscientious (Tob 4:18) and seek to be instructed by one who is wiser rather than you instead of following your own inclinations.

A good life makes you wise according to God, and expert in many things. The more humble you are in yourself, and more subject to God, the more prudent you will be in all things and then more at peace.

❦ 8 ❦

READING THE HOLY SCRIPTURES

Chapter 5 Focus: God wrote us a love letter! Read it and enjoy it. Read it over and over again. Don't worry too much about what ink color He used, or on what day He wrote His Letter to you and me. Write Him back, show Him you received His note via your daily actions.

This chapter puts a cap on the pursuit of knowledge, truth, and prudence.

Thomas loved Holy Scripture like a love letter. He copied it daily, memorized it, shared his knowledge of it, preached about it. He was immersed in Holy Scripture. We are certain that he copied the entire Bible (by hand) at least four times. What an example. He imitated Christ in that he was constantly mindful of Scripture. May we likewise imitate him. Good St. Jerome reportedly said that "Ignorance of Scripture is Ignorance of Christ." So don't be ignorant!

Thomas lays out the primary focus of Scripture - as he stated in Chapter 1, seeking the Truth. Thomas' good words about reading The Bible will help you think about your approach to reading God's Love Letter. Try the Lectio Divina method: Read, meditate, pray, and contemplate deeply upon the Word of God. You won't regret it. This method treats the Scriptures as the Living Word of God, not as texts to be studied.

Question: How does God speak to me in Scripture?

Chapter 5, In Short.

1. Truth is to be sought for in Holy Scripture.
2. God speaks the Truth to us in many ways with Holy Scripture.

THE TEXT ON READING THE HOLY SCRIPTURES

Seek the Truth in Holy Scripture, not in eloquence. All Holy Scripture ought to be read with the Spirit with which it was written. We must seek insight in the Scriptures rather than subtle expressions. We ought to read the devout and simple books as well as those that are high and profound.

Do not let the authority of the Scripture writer put you off from reading: it does not matter whether the author was of little or of great learning. Let the love of pure truth lead you to read deeply. Do not ask 'who said this?', but rather attend to what is said.

2. Everyone passes away, "but the truth of the Lord remains forever (Ps 117:2 & 1 Pt 1:25). " God speaks to us in many ways, regardless of our position in life. Our curiosity often hinders us in reading the Scriptures when we attempt to understand and discuss those passages which should simply be passed over.

Receive insight from this: read with humility, simplicity, and faith. Do not seek the fame of being learned in Scripture. Ask after the words of the saints and hear these with silence. Be pleased with the parables of the ancient ones, for such parables are told for a reason (Sr 3:29).

❅ 9 ❅

INORDINATE AFFECTIONS

Chapter 6 Focus: Can you have too much of a good thing? Well...Thomas tells us an obvious but difficult truth: We need more than bread - we need God's presence, His Word, in our lives. In this chapter, Thomas begins to reorient our desires from the worldly to the Godly.

If we eat too much, we will get indigestion; if we drink too much, we will suffer. Any "carnal" blessing can be perverted into a curse. The solution to the problem lies in controlling our desires and taking God-sized portions. We can shift our desires. "Man does not live by bread alone (Mt 4:4)."

Thomas advises us how to get out of our self-dug, self-indulgent hole: resist these passions by filling your desires with fruits of the Spirit for "against these, there is no law (Gal 5:23)".

It is just fine to enjoy a something so long as the desire for that item does not become unhealthy. God does not have laws against things in which we can "over indulge" such as love, joy, peace, patience, kindness, goodness, generosity, faithfulness, modesty, self-control, chastity (ibid). Of these, we can have as much as we want. Thomas tells us to let our passions be for these holy fruits.

Question: What passions have an unhealthy influence over my interior peace?

Chapter 6, In Short.

1. Desiring more than you should expect leads to restlessness.
2. True peace of the heart is found in resisting passions.

THE TEXT ON INORDINATE AFFECTIONS

Whenever you desire more than you should reasonably expect, you immediately become restless. The proud and the self-interested are never at rest, yet the poor in spirit and humble of heart abide in peace. Whoever is not wholly dead to the self is soon tempted and is overcome by small and unimportant things. It is hard for the weak in spirit to withdraw from all worldly desires, especially those who are still part of the carnal world and inclined to the pleasures of the flesh. When you withdraw from these attachments, you are often sad and easily angered if your desires are then thwarted.

2. On the other hand, if you yield to your tendencies, you are immediately weighed down by the conviction of your conscience. Following these desires, by yielding to them, you have not in any way achieved the hoped-for peace. **For true peace of the heart is to be found in resisting your passions, not in yielding to them.** When you are focused on the flesh there is no peace in your heart. Nor is there peace for you when you give up the struggle to the things that are outside of you. Peace rests with those who are fervent toward God and living in the life of the Spirit (Gal 5:16-25).

❧ 10 ❧

AVOIDING VAIN HOPE AND PRIDE

Chapter 7 Focus: And the winner of the prize for the most humble person goes to... Thomas offers us a warning and a promise: we face futility if we put our faith in anyone or anything other than God. However, God honors our efforts and intentions if the rationale for these is in accord with His Will.

Thomas invites us to build on our relationship with Almighty God. It is not that wealth or powerful friends are bad things, rather, we must keep these in perspective by putting God first. It is easy to think ourselves as not needing Him when we are in the flower of youth and health and wealth and popularity. But these talents are from God Himself. Think of Samson here (Jd 13-16). Thomas' admonition, then, is to stay humble in all of your efforts. With Christ as a model of humility, we can practice our humility and obtain peace and quiet strength.

Question: Do I glory in my position in life and count myself as "better" than others?

Chapter 7, In Short.

1. Life is vain for those who put trust in the children of Adam.
2. Take no glory in your riches or wealthy friends.

3. Be humble in your good works and do not count yourself as better than others.

THE TEXT ON AVOIDING VAIN HOPE AND PRIDE

Life is vain for those who put their trust in the children of Adam or in any created thing (Jr 17:5, Ps 146:2-4). Do not be ashamed to be the servant of others for the love of Jesus Christ, and to be reckoned as poor in this life (2 Cor 4:5).

Build your refuge in God (Ps 73:28), not upon your own capabilities. Do what is within your power and God will help your good intent. Trust in the favor of God, who resists the proud and gives grace to the humble (Lk 2). Do not trust in your learning, nor in the cleverness of others.

2. If you have wealth, take no glory in your riches. If you have powerful friends, do not rely on those relationships, but rely instead on your relationship with God, Who gives all things, and in addition to all things, He desires to give you even Himself (1 Cor 1:31).

It is futile to boast because of your strength or in the beauty of your body since it takes only a slight sickness for your health to fail and wither away. Do not take pride in your skillfulness or ability for fear that it will displease God, from Whom every good gift and talent which we have emanates.

3. **Do not count yourself better than others, since you will then be accounted worse in the sight of God, who knows what is in your heart.** Be humble about your good works, for God's judgments are of another sort than the judgments of man, and what pleases others is often displeasing to Him (Is 55:6-9).

If you have any good qualities, believe that others have even more admirable qualities than you, and so this way you may preserve your humility. There is no harm done to you if you place yourself below all others, but it is great harm if you place yourself above even the smallest person. Peace is always with the humble, but in the heart of the proud, there is envy and constant anger.

11

THE DANGERS OF FAMILIARITY

Chapter 8 Focus: What does it mean to be overly familiar? Thomas explains here why this trap needs to be avoided. It's that same notion involved with avoiding the near occasion of sin. We should carefully guard our hearts and our secrets. Thomas mentions flattery – a concept related to imitation. Often flattery is false and disingenuous, even ingratiating, whereas imitation is a true attempt at faithful mimicry. Our intimate conversations should be reserved for godly friends.

The language in this chapter was challenging in that it did not lend itself to direct equivalencies. This is because these admonitions were initially written for acolytes in a monastery. Luckily, Thomas gave us some biblical references to get a grip on what he was trying to teach us.

Questions: When have I been overly familiar to the point of committing sin? What situations cause me these temptations?

Chapter 8, In Short.

1. Handle your affairs with the wise and God-fearing.
2. Have a love for all, but do not be overly familiar.

THE TEXT ON THE DANGERS OF FAMILIARITY

"Open not your heart readily to anyone"(Sir 8:19), but handle your affairs with those who are wise and fear God. Keep regular company with mature people but not with strangers. Do not be a flatterer of the rich, nor willingly appear before the great. **Associate yourself with the humble and the simple, with the devout and the virtuous and occupy yourself with those things which build up one another (Rm 14:19).** Do not be overly familiar with a person of the opposite sex, but recommend them in their goodness, to God. Therefore, desire to be familiar only with God and His angels, and avoid the familiarity of others.

2. While we must have a love for all people, familiarity with everyone is not advisable. It sometimes happens that a person, when not known to us, shines by a good reputation, but then, when that person is present, is found to be disagreeable after all. Similarly, we sometimes think of pleasing others by our meeting with them; but then we actually repel them by the evil behavior which they discover in us.

12

OBEDIENCE AND SUBJECTION

Chapter 9 Focus: Our Lord Jesus Christ: Model of Obedience. The Creator of the universe humbled Himself to take on the form of a man, but first as a boy. This Boy learned a trade, washed dishes, fed the chickens, etc. His obedience and subjection are in cooperation with an authority even though that authority was not of those "superior" to Him: Mary and Joseph.

If we listen more, perhaps we will hear God more (Mt 17:5). Thomas calls us to an examination of our favorite opinions...our own. He's counseling us to keep our thoughts to ourselves and perhaps just to listen to those God has placed over us. You will hear His voice through those people God has placed in our lives.

In this chapter, Thomas self-reflects when he writes: "For I have often heard..." So he is taking his own advice. Encouraging.

Question: How can I practice obedience of mind, heart, and action?

Chapter 9, In Short.

1. It is a great thing to be under obedience.

2. Sometimes God teaches us to give up our own opinions for the sake of peace.

3. It is safer to listen and to take counsel than to give it.

THE TEXT ON OBEDIENCE AND SUBJECTION

It is a very great thing to be under obedience (Lk 2:51), to live under a superior and not be at our own disposal. It is a much more secure thing to be in a state of subjection than in a state of authority. Many are under obedience more because they have to be so for the love of God. People such as these are in pain and grumble easily. Nor will they gain freedom of mind unless they submit themselves with their whole heart for God's sake. Running here or there, you will find no rest, but only when you, in humble subjection, come under the rule of a superior. Be careful: Many have been deceived by imagining changing places with that person in authority.

2. It is true that people desire to act according to their own liking, and you are more likely to be in favor of your own opinions than those of others. But if God is among us, we sometimes must give up our own opinions for the sake of peace. **Who among us is so wise as to be able to know all things?** Therefore, do not trust your own thoughts too much, but be willing to hear the sentiments of others. Although your opinion may be good, yet if for God's sake you leave your own view behind to follow that of another it will be more beneficial to you.

3. For I have often heard that it is safer to take counsel and to listen than to give it. It may also happen that each one's thoughts may be good, but it is a sign of your pride and willfulness when you refuse to yield to others when reason or a just cause requires it.

⚘ 13 ⚘
AVOIDING A SUPERFLUITY OF WORDS

Chapter 10 Focus: Now that we've learned the purpose and benefit of obedience (Chapter 9) we can put that obedience into practice, along with the prudence we learned (Chapter 4), by controlling our tongues. So what's a talker to do (I am raising my hand)? Thomas advises us to use our words sparingly and carefully. Stay away from idle chatter. We should not enter into conversations that are not worth much, or that devolve into gossip. I think Thomas struggled with this as well since he states that "Oftentimes I wish I had been silent..."

But Thomas overcame this tendency when he advises us to "Watch and Pray". Not only because it is from Christ, but because if you are praying, you aren't talking to others: you are in conversation with God. Praying affords an opportunity to be present to the Lord. And the Lord will help us fill up that "void," with Himself. Letting my "yes" be "yes" and "no" be "no" keeps things simple (Mt 5:37). Why are we always explaining everything? It is not always necessary or helpful to explain our every thought. Keep words to a minimum. It's an exercise of a new habit. Try it out and see what He does when you talk to Him. Talk with God a lot, speak to His creatures a little.

Questions: How can I talk more with God?

How can I make my speech with others more meaningful and edifying?

Chapter 10, In Short.

1. Talking of worldly matters, even with good intentions, will hinder your spiritual life.

2. Devout conversations concerning spiritual matters help advance our spiritual progress.

THE TEXT ON AVOIDING A SUPERFLUITY OF WORDS

Flee the commotion of others as much as you can. Talking about worldly affairs, regardless of your good intention, will hinder your spiritual life. This is because we are quickly defiled and ensnared with vanity.

Oftentimes I wish I had been silent and not been in the company of others. But why are we so willing to talk and debate with one another, since we seldom return to silence without upsetting our conscience?

The reason why we are so willing to talk is because by talking with one another we seek comfort from one another. When we are wearied by various worldly thoughts, we gladly prefer to ease the heart this way. And we are very willing to talk and think of those things that we most love and desire, or when we imagine the ephemeral things that are working against us.

2. But, alas! It is often in vain and to no purpose: for this external comfort is a significant hurdle to your interior and divine consolation. Therefore, we must each "watch and pray (Mt 26:41)" that our time may not pass away without fruit. If you must speak, speak quickly, and speak of those things of God which build you up. **The neglect of our spiritual advancement, along with our bad habits, is a great cause of our keeping so little watch upon our mouth.** But devout conversations concerning spiritual matters help advance us toward spiritual progress, especially where those of the same mind and spirit are united together in God.

14

ACQUIRING PEACE AND ZEAL FOR OUR SPIRITUAL PROGRESS.

Chapter 11 Focus: We move from controlling our tongues to controlling our vices and bad habits. When we put God first, asking Him to join in our battle against our vices and passions, we will find peace along God's path for us. Taking inventory of our self includes looking at our unhealthy desires, and willing to be accountable for our words and deeds. Let's pledge, starting today, to gain control of these distasteful elements of our nature. These skirmishes will prepare us for when we are truly challenged to fight the real battles later on.

One of my favorite quotes of this book comes from this Chapter: "If every year we rooted out one vice, we would soon become perfect." Ultimately, for me, that one vice, if I can get to its tangled roots, will help me see that the remaining vices are small weeds indeed.

Question: What one vice can I root out this year?

Chapter 11, In Short.

1. Blessed are the single-hearted, for they shall enjoy much peace.

2. The Saints were able to cling to God by subduing their earthly desires.

3. We will be able to relish divine things when we are perfectly dead to ourselves.

4. The Lord is ready to help those who fight against such passions and trust in His grace.

5. If every year we rooted out one vice, we would soon become perfect.

6. Resist your inclinations now; break off bad habits, so that small faults will not grow.

THE TEXT ON ACQUIRING PEACE AND ZEAL FOR OUR SPIRITUAL PROGRESS.

We would have much peace if we were not so busy with the sayings and doings of others and with caring about those things which do not concern us. How can you remain peaceful for long when you entangle yourself with other peoples' cares, seeking events abroad, or being little or seldom inwardly reflective? Blessed are the single-hearted, for they shall enjoy much peace.

2. What was the reason why some of the Saints were so perfect and contemplative? Because they made it their sole study to subdue all earthly desires in themselves, and thus they were enabled, with every fiber of their heart, to cleave to God, and freely attend to themselves.

We are often occupied too much with our own passions, and too interested in transitory things. We seldom perfectly overcome so much as one habit nor are we earnestly bent upon our daily progress, and therefore we remain cold and tepid.

3. If we were perfectly dead to ourselves, and in no way inwardly entangled, then we might be able to relish divine things and experience something of heavenly contemplation. Our whole and greatest hindrance is that we are not free from worldly passions and lusts. We do not strive to walk in the perfect way of the saints. And when we do meet with any small adversity we are too quickly dispirited and then we turn away to seek after human comforts.

If we place our progress solely in these outward religious observances our devotion will quickly be at an end. So let us lay the ax at the root that, being purged of passions, we may possess a quiet mind.

4. If we strove like valiant soldiers to stand up in the battle, we would doubtlessly see our Lord help us from heaven. For He is ready to

help those who fight and trust in His grace: Who furnishes us with occasions of combat that we may overcome these obstacles.

5. **If every year we rooted out one vice, we would soon become perfect.** But now we often find it quite the other way around: that we were more pure and better in the beginning of our conversion than after many years of our profession of faith. Our fervor and progress ought to be greater every day, but now it is considered a great matter if a disciple can merely retain some part of that beginner's fervor. If we would use a little discipline on ourselves, in the beginning, we might afterward do all things with ease and joy.

6. It is hard to quit our old habits, but harder to go against our own will. But if you do not overcome things that are small and easy, when will you overcome even greater difficulties?

Resist your inclinations now, in the beginning, and break off your evil habits, lest perhaps, little by little, your difficulties will increase. Oh, if you were sensible, you would bring peace to yourself and joy to others. By behaving well yourself you will then be more eager for your own spiritual progress.

☙ 15 ❧

THE UTILITY OF ADVERSITY

Chapter 12 Focus: Our adversity has utility: bringing us closer to one another, closer to humility, and closer to the Lord. Indeed, why do we pray, do good works, go to Mass, write blogs about the Faith, protest abortion, etc.? It certainly does NOT make us the wunderkind of the community. These activities usually bring us derision, and so we "offer it up" for our own sins, and "those of the whole world."

Thomas tells us that we should place our hope in the Lord. While we may believe that someday the lion and the lamb will lay down together right now we will continue to have tribulation in this world. So we keep standing up for the rights of the unborn, the poor, the widow, the orphan, even in the face of the seeming futility because in this adversity a flag is raised to give others hope since He has overcome the world (Jn 16:33).

Question: What adversity do I face and how is this helping me to grow in my faith?

Chapter 12, In Short.

1. It is good for you to have some troubles and adversities.

2. Establish yourself in God so that you will not need to seek comfort from others.

THE TEXT ON THE UTILITY OF ADVERSITY

It is good for you to have some troubles and adversities, for as a disciple, these make you enter into yourself, so that you may know that you are in a state of banishment, and so that you may not place your hopes in anything of this world.

It is good that sometimes you suffer derision and that there are those who have an evil or imperfect opinion of us even when you do good things and intend good things. These adversities are often a help to you in the practicing of humility and defending yourselves against conceit. When outwardly we are despised by our enemies and given little credit it is much easier to run to our inward Witness, who is God.

2. As a disciple, therefore, you should root yourself in God in such a way as to have no need of seeking comforts from others. **When a disciple of good will is troubled, or tempted, or afflicted with evil thoughts, then it is easier to understand the need for God, without Whom you can do no good (Jn 15:5).** The disciple then also laments, sighs, and prays, by reason of the miseries suffered. Weary of living longer, and wishing death to come, the disciple prays to be "depart this life and be with Christ (Phil 1:23)." The disciple then comes to the realization that perfect security and full peace cannot be found in this world.

❦ 16 ❦

RESISTING TEMPTATIONS

Chapter 13 Focus: We are faced with temptation all of our life. We must pay attention to our temptations because these teach us about our path to holiness. Even the best of saints, like St. Francis of Assisi, were frequently tempted. Legend has it that St. Francis would roll in the snow when tempted toward lust, or throw himself into thorn bushes! The Book of Hebrews asks us if we have resisted to the point of shedding blood (Heb 12:4). Maybe that's what he was after. I can't say that I have ever went to that level to resist a temptation.

I like how Thomas points out that some disciples face their temptations at the beginning of their conversion, others at the end of their journey: notice that we all face temptations!

Getting to the root of the temptation is the key to conquering whatever is vying for our attention. We must use these events as an opportunity to grow in faith. We must use the Confessional to seek Reconciliation with God.

Question: What are my temptations and how can I ask God to help me overcome these to profit spiritually?

Chapter 13, In Short.

1. We cannot be without troubles and temptations.

2. Temptations are troublesome but spiritually profitable.

3. You are never secure from temptations as long as you live.

4. The beginning of all temptations is instability of temper and lack of trust in God.

5. Many disciples suffer their worst temptations at the beginning of their conversion, some at the end.

6. Do not despair when tempted, but cry out to God for a way to escape or bear it.

7. Temptations and troubles show your spiritual progress.

THE TEXT ON RESISTING TEMPTATIONS

As long as we live in this world we cannot be without tribulation and temptation. And so it is written in the Book of Job: "the life of a man upon earth is a temptation and a drudgery" (Job 7:1). Everyone, therefore, ought to be anxious about his temptations and to watch in prayer, for fear that the devil, who never sleeps but "goes about seeking whom he may devour," might find room to deceive him (1 Peter 5:8). **No one is so perfect and holy as not to have some temptations, and we never can be wholly free from them.**

2. Although troublesome and regretful, temptations are often very profitable to you; for in these you are humbled, purified, and instructed. The saints have passed through many tribulations and temptations and have profited by the same. Those who could not overcome their temptations have become condemned and fallen away. There is no order so holy, nor a place so remote, where there are no temptations or adversities.

3. You are never entirely secure from temptations as long as you live, because we have within us the source of temptation, having been born with a sinful nature. When one temptation or troubling thought is over, another comes on, and we shall have always something to suffer because we have lost the goodness of our original happiness.

Likewise, many who seek to flee temptations fall more painfully into them. We cannot overcome temptations by flight alone, but by patience and true humility we are made stronger than our enemies. Whoever only fights off temptations outwardly and does not pluck out its root will profit little. Indeed, temptations will soon return to you and you will find yourself in a worse situation than before.

By degree, and by patience, with forbearance, you shall by God's grace better overcome temptation than by the harshness of your own demands. In temptation, often take counsel from others, and do not deal harshly with anyone who is tempted, but comfort them as you would wish to be comforted.

4. The beginning of all temptations to evil is instability of temper and lack of trust in God. Even as a ship without a rudder is tossed about by the waves, so are those who are careless and infirm of purpose tempted, now on this side, now on that. As fire tests iron, so does temptation test the upright (Prov 27:7).

We oftentimes do not know what strength we have, but temptation reveals to us what really we are. Nevertheless, we must watch, especially in the beginnings of temptation; for then is the foe the more easily mastered. We must meet the devil outside the door as soon as the enemy's knock is heard rather than allow the thought enter within our mind.

Wherefore one says,

"Withstand the beginnings; once you might've have cured,

But now 'tis past your skill, too long has it endured."

For first comes to the mind the simple suggestion, then strong imagination, then pleasure, then evil affection, then assent.

And so little by little the enemy enters in altogether, because of your failure to resist at the beginning. And the longer you delay your resistance, the weaker you grow, and the stronger the enemy grows against you.

5. Some disciples suffer their worst temptations at the beginning of their conversion, some at the end. Some are sorely tried their whole life long. There are some who are only mildly tempted, according to the wisdom and justice of the ordering of God, Who knows your character and circumstances, and orders all things for the welfare of His elect.

6. Therefore we ought not to despair when we are tempted. Rather, we should cry out to God more fervently in order that He will grant us help in all our tribulation. And we should pray that He will, as St. Paul

says, make a way to escape the temptation or that we may be able to bear it (1 Cor 10:13). Let us, therefore, humble ourselves under the mighty Hand of God in all temptation and trouble, for He will save and exalt those who are humble of spirit.

7. It is easy to be devout and zealous when you are not under temptation or adversity. If you act with patience during such affliction though, then you have the potential for great spiritual progress. Some are kept safe from great temptations but are overtaken by those little and common occurrences, such that any resulting humiliation may teach them not to trust themselves in great things, being weak in small things.

❧ 17 ❧

AVOIDING RASH JUDGMENT

Chapter 14 Focus: Our judgments of others are biased - driven by our hard hearts and sinful prejudices. Seldom do we attempt to understand the other person's position or situation. We are right! They are wrong! They must be evil!

We often condemn the actions of others what we would ordinarily ignore or approve of ourselves. We put on blinders with respect to our own defects. But it is we who are sinning in our position of judgment. And so long as things are going well, we can keep up the pretense of ignorance and normalcy.

Thomas's remedy is to rely on the power of Christ.

For there God takes our reason and magnifies the love for Him towards our neighbor.

Question: What measures can I put in place to avoid judging others?

Chapter 14, In Short.

1. Beware that you do not judge the actions of others.

2. Some secret thought often lurks within us, turning us aside.

3. It is not easy to see with the eyes of another.

THE TEXT ON AVOIDING RASH JUDGMENT

Beware that you do not judge the actions of others. In judging others you labor in vain; you often err, and you easily fall into sin. It is in judging and examining yourself that you labor to good purpose.

As a matter touches our fancy, we often judge it accordingly. Because of our own personal feelings, we can easily fail at the measure of true judgment. **If God were always the sole object of our desire, we would be less troubled by the erring judgment of our fancy.**

2. But often there is some secret thought lurking within us, or even some outward circumstance, which turns us aside. Many secretly seek their own ends in what they do, yet do not know it. They seem to live with good peace of mind so long as things go well for them, and according to their desires, but once these desires are frustrated and broken, immediately they are shaken and displeased. The diversity of feelings and opinions very often brings about dissensions between friends, between countrymen, between the devout and godly.

3. Established custom is not easily given over. And it is not easy to see with the eyes of another. If you rely more on your own reason or experience than upon the power of Jesus Christ, your light shall come slowly and meekly. For God wills us to be perfectly subject to Himself, and all our reason to be exalted by abundant love towards Him.

18

WORKS OF CHARITY

Chapter 15 Focus: Our actions are pleasing to God when done for the pure intent of satisfying His Will and for His Glory. Thomas cautions us that our faith can become weak when not accompanied by good works. Those who have true charity (love), have truly learned that all else, again, is vanity.

Question: Does my faith show through my good works?

> Chapter 15, In Short.
> 1. Nothing must be done that is evil.
> 2. Whoever does much, loves much.
> 3. Whoever has true charity desires that only glory for God.

THE TEXT ON WORKS OF CHARITY

Nothing must be done that is evil even if done for the love of another or for worldly good. Sometimes a good work must be postponed, or be altered in order to help those suffering. In this way, a good work is not destroyed but finished.

No work has its benefits without love, but whatever is done in charity (love), regardless of how small and lowly, brings forth good fruit. For God always considers what you are able to do, more than the greatness of what you have done.

2. **Whoever does much, loves much.** Those who do much, do well (Js 2:14 ff). Those who do well minister to the public good rather than to their own self-interest. Oftentimes that which seems to be charity is really carnality, because the charitable work springs from your natural inclinations toward self-will, the hope of repayment, and desire for gain.

3. Whoever has true and perfect charity, does not seek their own good but desires that God alone be glorified. No one is envied here because there is no longing for selfish joy. Likewise, you have no desire to rejoice in yourself, but rather you long to receive God's blessing as the highest good. Ascribe to praise God alone. He is the Fountain from which all goodness flows and as the End, the Peace, and the Joy of all Saints. Oh, you who have but a spark of true charity, have truly learned that all worldly things are full of vanity.

19

BEARING THE FAULTS OF OTHERS

Chapter 16 Focus: There is nothing wrong with pursuing correct behavior, attitudes, and obedience for ourselves. However, unless God says otherwise, we need to put up with the shortcomings of others. We don't like it much when we are criticized for our own faults. But we tend to like it a little too much when we get to point out the faults of others. This is Thomas' point. And it dovetails well with chapter 14 and 15.

Thomas tells us that God makes us aware of the faults of others in order help us see our own shortcomings and help us to draw nearer to Him. In supporting each other and bearing with one another, we will seek Him out all the more. Such adversity proves us ready to be open to His correction(s). Now, multiply that.

Question: How can I bear with the faults of others?

Chapter 16, In Short.

1. We ought to bear with the faults of others.

2. Why is it that we are ready to see others made perfect, and yet we do not amend our own imperfections?

3. We want others corrected but are not willing to accept correction ourselves.

4. Since no one is without defect, God wishes us to bear with one another.

THE TEXT ON BEARING WITH THE FAULTS OF OTHERS

Those things which you cannot amend in yourself or in others, you ought patiently to bear, until God demands otherwise. Do you think that perhaps it is better for your trial and patience, without which our merits are but of little worth? Nevertheless, you ought to beseech God, when you find such impediments, that He would sustain you so that you are able to bear these faults with good will.

2. If one who is once or twice admonished refuses to listen, do not argue about it, but commit this all to God, that His will may be done and His honor is shown in His servants: For He knows well how to convert the evil into good (Gn 50:20; 45:4-8).

Try to be patient in bearing with one another's faults and infirmities whatever they may be, for you yourself have many defects which others have to put up with. **If you cannot make your own self what you desire, how can you correct another to your own liking?** We are ready to see others made perfect, and yet seldom do we amend our own shortcomings.

3. Likewise, we would have others strictly corrected, but we are not willing to be corrected ourselves. While the freedom of others displeases us, we are dissatisfied only when our own wishes are denied. We desire rules to be made restraining the conduct of others, but by no means will we permit ourselves to be restrained. Therefore it plainly appears how seldom we weigh down our neighbor in the same balance as ourselves. If everyone was perfect, then what would we have to suffer from others for God?

4. But now God has ordained that we ought to learn to bear one another's burdens, because no one is without defect, none without a burden, none sufficient, none wise enough. Yet it benefits us all to bear with one another, to comfort one another, to help, instruct, and admonish one another. How much strength you have is proved best by occasions of adversity. Such occasions do not make you frail but show what mettle you are made of.

✤ 20 ✤

THE CONSECRATED DISCIPLE

Chapter 17 Focus: Thomas lays out the simple path to a consecrated life. While this was written with the title "On the Religious or Monastic Life," I renamed it since today few of us will ever make such a life commitment. It was very common in his time for many men and women to choose (or default to) a religious life. However, Thomas' ancient advice is still valid for us since he is addressing the full consecration of the disciple. This was one reason for the fictional narrative in the front of this book.

In walking this path toward following Christ we must turn away from worldly obsessions. The fundamental change in our character is shown with evidence of an increased humility. These changes are not a competition, but rather choices made to deepen our love for God. Our focus must be therefore, upon God.

Questions: Have I consecrated my life to God?
What evidence do I have of this consecration?

Chapter 17, In Short.

1. In order to lead a Christ-centered life, be ready to be counted as a fool for Christ.

2. A person of faith is marked by good character and has discipline over their worldly affections.

3. Disciples must humble themselves with all their heart for the love of God.

THE TEXT ON THE RELIGIOUS OR MONASTIC LIFE

You must learn to renounce your own will in many things if you will live in peace and order with others. It is no small thing to belong to a faith community or congregation, and to live there without complaint, remaining faithful in it until the day of your death (Mt 10:22).

Blessed are you who have lived a good life in such a community, and brought it to a happy end. If you will stand fast and benefit as you ought, hold yourself out as an exile and a pilgrim upon the earth (Heb 11:13). **If you are to lead a Christ-centered life, you will have to be counted as a fool for Christ.**

2. Your clothing and outward appearance are of little importance (Mt 6:28). It is a change of character and a full mortification of worldly affections which make you truly a person of faith.

3. Whoever seeks anything other than God and the salvation of his soul, shall find only trouble and sorrow. Nor can anyone stand long in peace, who do not strive to be the least of all and the servant of all. You came here to serve, not to govern. You are called to work and struggle, not to a life of ease and idle talk. Here then, disciples are tried as gold in the furnace. No one can remain here unless they are willing to humble themselves with all their heart for the love of God.

✺ 21 ✺

THE EXAMPLE OF THE HOLY FATHERS

Chapter 18 Focus: Thomas takes the opportunity to distinctly praise the early Church leaders. Because there was a Papal schism during his time, great unrest hovered over the Church: the role of the clergy was inconsistent due to inadequate teaching and poor training for those in the consecrated life. These troubles, following on the heels of the Black Plague (and its frequent, smaller outbreaks) made for unsettling times. The faith of the people was shaken, and the Church had few answers to adequately address these crises. So Thomas looks to the misty past for his heroes.

These early Church leaders are excitedly praised for their toughness and holiness even during rampant persecutions. The lesson to us is that imitating the imitators brings us that much closer to Christ. These imitators were the early Church Fathers who laid the foundations of the faith. Most of these theologians were taught by the Apostles and set the foundations of early Christianity through their thoughts, deeds, and influence. Many were martyred, and many sainted.

Thomas' appreciation for their influence is laid out in this chapter as an example for us today. By enduring privations and imitating these patriarchs of the Church, we imitate Christ. He holds up these icons as great examples to us all. He calls us to deeper prayer and warns of the dangers of slothful behavior and a tepid devotion.

Question: Who are the models of faith for you?

Chapter 18, In Short.

1. Follow the examples of the Saints.
2. Those who would walk in the footsteps of Christ must endure many tribulations.
3. The devout spent their time seeking moments alone with God.
4. The Saints were precious and beloved in the sight of God.
5. In the beginning of this sacred institution the devout were loved.
6. Because of sloth and lukewarmness, life is becoming difficult.

THE TEXT ON THE EXAMPLE OF THE HOLY FATHERS

Consider now the lively examples of the holy fathers, in whom real devotion and perfection showed forth, and you shall see how little it is that we do, adding up to nothing. Ah! What is our life when compared with theirs? Saints and friends of Christ as they were, they served the Lord in hunger and thirst, in cold and nakedness, in labor and weariness, in watching and fasting, in prayer and holy meditations, in persecutions and many reproaches (Heb 11:37).

2. O how many and serious trials the Apostles, Martyrs, Confessors, Virgins, did endure. All others who want to walk in the footsteps of Christ should be prepared to endure the same. For they despised their souls in this world that they might keep their souls preserved for eternal life (Jn 12:25).

O how strict and retired a life was that of the holy fathers who dwelt in the desert! What long and dreadful temptations they did suffer! How often they were assaulted by the enemy! What frequent and fervid prayers did they offer unto God! What strict fasts did they endure! What fervent zeal and desire after spiritual profit did they manifest! How bravely did they fight so that their vices might not gain mastery over them! How entirely and persistently did they pursue God! By day they labored, and at night they gave themselves over to frequent prayer; yes, even when they were at work they continued in mental prayer.

3. They spent their whole time profitably. Every hour with God seemed short, and, through the great sweetness of contemplation, even the need of bodily rest was put aside. They renounced all riches, dignities, honors, friends, and kinsmen. They desired nothing from the world. They ate the bare necessities of life: it pained them to minister to their own personal needs, and even of the necessities of the body. Thus they were poor in earthly things, but rich in the heavenly measures of grace and virtue. Though poor to the outer eye, within they were filled with grace and heavenly favor.

4. They were strangers to the world, but to God, they were as kinsmen and friends. They seemed to themselves as having no reputation and in the world's eyes contemptible, but in the sight of God, they were precious and beloved.

They stood fast in true humility; they lived in simple obedience; they walked in love and patience, and thus they grew strong in spirit and obtained great favor before God. To all the devout, they were offered as an example, and they ought to motivate us more to good living rather than to promote the popular notions toward lukewarm temptations and a life of carelessness.

5. O how great was the love of all the devout at the beginning of this sacred institution! O what devoted prayer! What rivalry in holiness! What strict discipline was observed! What reverence and obedience they showed in all things under the rule of the Master! The traces of them that remain until now testify that they were truly holy and perfect disciples, who fighting so bravely trod the world underfoot. Now a disciple is only counted great when not counted as a transgressor, and as one who patiently endures that task which was undertaken.

6. O the coldness and negligence of our times: we are so quick to diminish from the former love, and because of sloth and lukewarmness it becomes wearisome to live. **Would to God that advancement in virtue was not completely asleep in those of you who have so often seen so many examples of the devout!**

❧ 22 ❧

THE SPIRITUAL EXERCISE OF THE DEVOUT DISCIPLE

Chapter 19 Focus: Spiritual exercises help us to get strong and to stay healthy in our faith walk of prayer, fasting, corporal and spiritual works of mercy, and so on. Everyone has different needs and capabilities in this area. Thomas calls us to be transparent in our spiritual progress, and gives us a prayer to get started.

These exercises are not to be carelessly set aside. The right exercises will help us to develop "spiritual muscles" in all the right places, especially in warding off our favorite temptations.

Finally, when the calendar rolls to especially holy seasons, (think Advent, Christmas, Lent, Easter), we should adjust and increase our spiritual practices in accordance with these seasons.

This chapter contains a quote for which Thomas is often cited, another favorite of mine: **Man proposes but God disposes.** In the spiritual life, this simply means that when we are set to try something, or achieve some new goal or execute some ingenious plan, many other items pop up to keep us from accomplishing that task. Still, we should step up our efforts and be bold. God is not mocking us, only directing us toward the work that is His will.

Question: How can I strengthen my spiritual muscles?

Chapter 19, In Short.

1. Let your outward life reflect your inward life.

2. The rate of your spiritual progress is determined according to your goals; remember, however, that "Man proposes but God disposes."

3. Do not omit spiritual exercises.

4. Make time to examine yourself twice daily, identifying your temptations.

5. If you have leisure time, use it for self-directed devotion.

6. Prepare for the solemn seasons by prayerful renewal.

7. Blessed is that servant, whom, when the Lord comes, He shall find watching.

THE TEXT ON THE SPIRITUAL EXERCISE OF THE DEVOUT DISCIPLE

The Christian life ought to be adorned with all virtues. We should, therefore, be inwardly what we demonstrate outwardly to others. And truly we should be even better within than without, for God is a discerner of our hearts, Whom we must reverence with all our hearts wherever we are, and walk pure in His presence as do the angels. Daily we ought to renew our vows and to kindle our hearts to zeal, as if each day were the first day of our conversion, and to say to Him,

> *"Help me, O God, in my good resolutions, and in Your holy service, and grant that this day I may make a good beginning, for prior to this I have done nothing!"*

2. The rate of our spiritual progress is determined according to our resolution. Likewise, diligence is required for those who would make good progress. It is better if you resolve bravely and yet fall short than to make rare or feeble resolutions and do nothing.

But many things happen to bring about the abandonment of our resolution - yet even a trivial omission of holy exercises can hardly be made without recognizing some loss to us. The resolution of the righteous depends more upon the grace of God than upon their own wisdom. The righteous always put their trust in Him, no matter what comes to their hands. **For man proposes, but God disposes.** And the way of a man is not in himself (Jr 10:23).

3. If spiritual exercises are sometimes omitted for the sake of some pious act, or by some act of kindness, it can easily be taken up later. But if these practices are neglected simply because of your discomfort or laziness, then this is sinful and harmful.

No matter how hard we strive, we will still fall short in many things. We should always make some distinct resolution, and, most of all, we must strive against those sins which most easily beset us. Both our outer and inner life should be thoroughly examined and ruled by us because both are concerned with our progress.

4. If you cannot always be examining your conscience, you can do so at appointed times, at least twice per day, at evening and at morning. In the morning, make your resolutions, and in the evening inquire into your life, how you have spent today in word, deed, and thought. In these ways, you have often possibly offended God and your neighbor.

Gird up your loins against the assaults of the devil. Bridle your appetites and you will soon be able to bridle every inclination of the flesh. Never be completely idle, but be doing something: be it reading, or writing, or praying, or meditating, or something useful to the community. Bodily exercises, however, must be undertaken with discretion, nor are these to be used by all in the same way.

5. The duties which are not common to all must not be done openly, but are most safe when carried on in secret. But take heed to not become careless in your common duties and more devout in secret, but faithfully and honestly discharge the duties and commands which fall to you. Afterward, if you still have leisure, then give yourself to yourself as your devotion leads you.

Not all can have the same exercise: one disciple is suited better to this measure and another to that one. At different seasons different exercises are needed, and some are suited better for feasts, some for fasts. We need one kind in time of peace and quietness and another in a time of temptation. Some are suitable to times of sadness, and others when we are joyful in the Lord (Ecc 3:1-14).

6. When we draw near the time of the great feasts, good exercises

should be renewed, and the prayers of the holy ones more fervently sought out. We ought to make our resolutions from one Feast to another as if each season were the period of our departure from this world and of entering into the Eternal Feast. So we ought to prepare ourselves fervently during the solemn seasons, and likewise live more solemnly. We should keep the purest watch on each holy observance, as though we were soon to receive the reward of our labors at the Hand of God.

7. And if this is deferred, let us believe ourselves to be ill-prepared and not yet worthy of the glory which shall be revealed to us at the appointed season, and let us study to prepare ourselves better for our life's end. Blessed is that servant, as the Evangelist Luke has it, whom, when the Lord comes He shall find watching. "Truly, I say to you He will make him ruler over all that He has (Lk 12:43, 44)."

✣ 23 ✣

THE LOVE OF SOLITUDE AND SILENCE

Chapter 20 Focus: Pursuing solitude and silence is a worthy effort, especially if done for prayerful engagement. So how do we set aside those distractions? When we look at the Saints and how they model virtue, we will find them in solitude, in quiet meditation. To be sure, this is a challenge, but sometimes communing with the Almighty is as simple as going to your room and closing the door. Try it!

Question: Do I set aside time for quiet prayer?

Chapter 20, In Short.

1. Set aside the time and place for meditation and prayer.

2. Pursuing outside interests, makes it difficult to remain meditative and prayerful.

3. Look to the Saints for models of virtue.

4. Take great care in staying humble and denying the world in order to stay in God's grace.

5. You will find solace and intimacy with God in contemplating Him privately.

6. Studying Scripture and dropping meaningless relationships advances you in the spiritual life.

7. Do not exchange spiritual focus for worldly pleasures.

8. Leave vain things to vain people, and mind the things which God has commanded you.

THE TEXT ON THE LOVE OF SOLITUDE AND SILENCE

Seek a suitable time for your meditation, and think frequently of God's mercies to you. Leave aside your curious questions. Study such matters as bring you sorrow for your sin rather than for amusement. If you withdraw yourself from trifling conversations and idle visits, as well as from silly novelties and gossip, you should find sufficient time for good meditation. The greatest Saints, as far as they were able, avoided the company of others and chose instead to live in secret with God.

2. It has been said, "As often as I have gone among men, so often have I returned less a man." (Attributed to Seneca.) This is what we often experience when we linger in our conversations. It is easier to be silent than it is to be frugal with words. It is easier to remain hidden at home than to keep sufficient guard upon yourself abroad. Whoever, therefore, seeks to reach that which is hidden and spiritual, must go with Jesus "apart from the multitude" (Mk 7:33; Lk 22:6).

No one safely goes abroad who does not love to rest at home.

No one safely talks except those who love to remain silent and at peace.

No one safely rules but those who love to be subject to others.

No one safely commands but those who love to obey.

3. Those who have the testimony of a good conscience safely rejoice. The boldness of the Saints was always full of the fear of God. Those Saints stood out with great virtue and grace and yet remained humble and earnest in themselves. But the boldness of the wicked springs from pride and presumption and, at the last, turns to their own confusion. Never promise yourself security in this life, no matter how sincere a believer you are or how devout you seem.

4. Often those who are held in the high esteem of others experience a more serious fall from grace because of their great overconfidence.

It may simply be better for some to be not altogether free from temptations. It may simply be better for them to be tempted often so that they do not become over confident. Otherwise, they may become too lifted up with pride or else lean too freely upon the consolations of the world.

O how good a conscience should be kept by the disciple, who never became entangled with the world! This is one who never sought a joy that passes away. O disciple of God, how great peace and quiet you will possess, when you cast off all vain cares, and think only of wholesome and divine things, building your whole hope upon God!

5. No one is worthy of heavenly consolation except those who have diligently practiced holy compunction. If you will feel this remorse within your heart, then enter into your room and shut out the noise of the world. For it is written: "Commune within your own heart in your own room and be still (Ps 4:5)."

In retiring to your room you will find that which you often lose abroad. If you continue this practice, such retirement there grows sweet, but if you do not keep to it, it becomes wearisome. If in the beginning of your conversation, you dwell in your room and keep it well, afterward it shall be a dear friend to you and offer a most pleasant solace.

6. In silence and quiet, the devout soul goes forward and learns the hidden things of the Scriptures. There you will find a fountain of tears, where you can wash and cleanse yourself each night. Then you may grow dearer to your Maker as you dwell further away from all worldly distraction (Ps 6).

God, with His holy angels, will draw near to the disciple who withdraws from acquaintance and friends. It is better to be unknown and pay attention to yourself than to neglect yourself and work wonders. It is commendable for a devout person to seldom travel abroad, to escape from being seen, and to have no desire to see others.

7. Why do you look at what you may not have? "Yet the world and its enticements are passing away (1 Jn 2:17)." The desires of sensuality draw you abroad, but, when an hour is past, what do you bring home but more weight upon your conscience and distraction of heart?

A merry going forth often brings a sorrowful return, and a merry evening makes a sad morning. So, while all carnal pleasures may begin pleasantly, ultimately these end in decay and destruction. What can you see abroad which you cannot see at home? Behold the heavens and the earth, and all the elements, for out of these are all things made.

8. What do you see anywhere around you which can continue long under the sun? You believe that you might be satisfied, but you will never be able to attain this pleasure. If you happen to see all things before you at once, what would it be but a vain vision (Lk 4:5-8)? Lift up your eyes to God on high, and pray that your sins and omissions may be forgiven (Eccl 1:4; Ps 123:1).

Leave vain things to vain people, and mind the things which God has commanded you. Shut your door behind you, and call out to Jesus your Beloved. Remain with Him in your chamber, for you will not find so great a peace anywhere else. If you had not gone out or listened to vain talk, you would be able to keep yourself in good peace. But since you are sometimes delighted at hearing new things, you must, therefore, suffer troubles of heart.

❄ 24 ❄

COMPUNCTION OF HEART

Chapter 21 Focus: Chapter 21 requires a few definitions. Compunction is a $50 word for the feeling of contrition, guilt, regret or sorrow for sin. It's a heart-based incident relating to your conscience. As negative as this sounds, these are actually positive notions of healing our soul. Contrition, regret, and a stirring of your conscience are worthwhile, especially when you are trying to improve yourself or, as in this meditation, coming to recognize the sadness behind our choice in rejecting God's love by choosing our favorite sins. In this role, compunction of heart is a path to holiness.

A second definition that needs clarification is "fear of God." In this writing, "fear of God" (and elsewhere "fear of the Lord") is a healthy, sovereign respect for the awesome nature of God. God is all powerful. Recognizing this power is similar to recognizing the power of a tornado or a bonfire - when you encounter such power, you become acutely aware your limits within its presence.

Thomas wants us to reflect upon our sins, our vices, our bad habits, and our pursuit of meaningless activity as a way to experience this profound sorrow. We should experience loss. We should grieve over our transgressions because, like the spurning of a lover, we have offended God. And while we deserve rejection in kind for our sinful commissions and omissions, instead, our Lord offers consolation and healing.

Thomas advises God's disciples to use this "holy compunction" as a path to reconciliation with Him. Through a serious reflection upon our shortcomings and sins, especially those sins of the past, we can pursue spiritual disciplines that will bring us closer to God's comfort and salvation now and in the future.

QUESTIONS: How do I show sorrow and repent for my sins.
How has this sorrow brought me closer to God?
Chapter 21, In Short.
1. Keep yourself in the fear of God in order to make spiritual progress.
2. We often do not recognize the sorrows of our own soul.
3. Stay away from the affairs of others.
4. We are all unworthy of divine consolation.
5. If you thought more about your death rather than the length of your life, you would strive to improve your life.
6. In spiritual poverty, we are easily lead to complaining.

THE TEXT ON COMPUNCTION OF HEART

In order to make any spiritual progress, keep yourself in the fear of God and never wish to be completely free (Prv 9:10). Use discipline in restraining all of your senses, and do not give yourself over to senseless amusements. Rather, find interior peace by focusing your reflection on heartfelt compunction.

Compunction opens the way for many good things, which is soon destroyed by intemperance. In this life, it is a wonder that anyone can ever rejoice fully when they consider and weigh their given banishment from God and the many dangers which beset their soul.

2. Because of our lightness of heart and neglect of our shortcomings, we do not recognize the sorrows of our own soul. We often laugh

vainly, when we should weep. There is no true liberty nor true joy except in the fear of God and in maintaining a good conscience.

You are happy when you can cast away every distraction and face up to holy compunction's one purpose. The happy put away whatever may stain or burden their conscience.

Strive courageously. Habit is overcome by habit. Do not make excuses that others hold you back. If you leave bad habits alone, they will gladly leave you alone to do the works that you must.

3. Stay away from the affairs of others. Do not entangle yourself with the business of the famous and powerful. Always keep your eye on yourself, and give advice to yourself rather than to your dearest friends.

If you do not have the favor of others, do not be cast down, but let your concern be that you do not regard yourself so highly and thoughtfully, as fitting a servant of God and devout disciple. It is often better and safer for a disciple to not have many comforts in this life, especially those which concern the flesh. When we do not seek compunction of heart we miss out on divine comforts or rarely feel these. In this case, we must blame ourselves or instead cast away those comforts which are vain and worldly.

4. Know that we are all unworthy of divine consolation, and instead are worthy only of tribulation. When a disciple has perfect compunction, the world is only burdensome and bitter.

A devout disciple finds sufficient cause for mourning and weeping. You know that no one lives on earth without suffering; neither you nor your neighbor, and the more thoroughly you look into your own heart, the more thoroughly you will grieve.

Within our sins and vices, there are grounds for real grief and inward contrition. We find ourselves so entangled in these sins that we are seldom able to contemplate heavenly things.

5. **If you thought more about your impending death rather than how long your life will be, you would eagerly strive to improve your life.** And if you seriously consider the future pains of hell and purgatory, I believe you would willingly endure such toil and pain now rather than facing the hardships of punishment. But because these things do not reach the heart, and we still love pleasant things, we remain cold and miserably indifferent.

6. In this spiritual poverty, our wretched bodies are lead easily to complaining. Therefore, pray humbly to the Lord that He will give you the spirit of compunction and say in the words of the Prophet, "Feed me, O Lord, with the bread of tears, and give me plenty of tears to drink (Ps 80:6)."

❧ 25 ❦

CONTEMPLATION OF THE MISERIES AND SORROWS OF THIS LIFE.

Chapter 22 Focus: In reading chapter 22, I'm reminded of a song from Gershwin's opera, "Porgy and Bess." Porgy sings "I got plenty O nuthin...and nuthin's plenty for me." I will probably ask my family to play this at my funeral. In the song, Porgy regales us with the convenience of being poor. He doesn't have to worry about locking his doors because he doesn't have anything worth stealing. He does have the sun, the moon and the deep blue sea, though. In the end, he's "got his gal, got his song, got his Lord. Give it a listen.

Because we live in the world we eat, sleep, work, love, play, suffer, etc. There is no denying this as part of the human condition. Without God at the center of our needs, life becomes a misery. We should adopt the attitude of Porgy and not have to "pray all the day" because of worrying about our things. He's just glad he's alive.

I always wonder how people without the gift of Faith in God make it through tough times. I wonder if those steeped in the material secretly pray to God to "keep the debble (devil) away," as Porgy says. Thomas takes up this point in noting that such needs are a constant source of weakness and temptation. No one has everything they need and certainly not everything they want.

If we do not get our simple desires under control the avenue to sin becomes paved with these desires. For example, when we see someone who we think has more than us or has an easier way than us, we slip into a position of envy - we are not happy with our lot. We need to be more like Porgy - "like the stars in de skies, all are free....ain't no use complainin'."

Thomas would agree, saying that we should be content with a modest amount of necessities. We should stay detached from the mentality of accumulation: that "plenty of plenty" Porgy sings about. Instead, we should work on our spiritual progress.

Many ignore their own spiritual progress, and would gladly wallow in the accumulation of their worldly goods. For others, breaking free from these desires can be accomplished with intentional self-discipline: It is never too late for this effort.

Thomas counsels us to return to the willing attitude we had at the beginning of our journey. We must remain open to instruction and be willing to grow in our faith. Like the words from another song of "Porgy and Bess," "Summer Time," "One of these mornings You're going to rise up singing, Then you'll spread your wings, And you'll take to the sky...."

Questions: What material things do I really need?

Do my possessions interfere with my relationship with God?

Chapter 22, In Short:

1. Turn to God or you will be miserable.

2. Your happiness does not lie in the abundance of worldly things.

3. The inwardly focused are too burdened with the necessities of the body.

4. The foolish and faithless of heart are buried deep in worldly things.

5. Do not lose your desire to progress in spiritual things.

6. The frailty of mortals is great because we are always prone to evil.

7. What shall become of us in the end, if at the beginning we are lukewarm?

THE TEXT ON THE CONTEMPLATION OF THE MISERIES AND SORROWS OF THIS LIFE.: ON THE NECESSITIES OF LIFE BECOMING A JOYLESS BURDEN WITHOUT GOD.

Unless you turn to God you will be miserable no matter where you are, and no matter where you turn. Why are you worried if a thing does not happen to you according to your wishes and desires? Do you know anyone who has everything according to his will? Neither I, nor you, nor any disciple upon the earth has this. There is no one in the world free from trouble or anguish, not even the King or the Pope. Who is it who has the happiest lot? The disciple who is strong is willing to offer such suffering for God.

2. There are many foolish and unstable people who say, "See what a prosperous life that one has - how rich and how great, how powerful, how exalted." But lift up your eyes to the good things of heaven, and you shall see that all these worldly things are nothing, they are utterly uncertain, yes, they are wearisome, because these things are never possessed without care and fear. The happiness of a disciple does not lie in the abundance of temporal things: a moderate portion will suffice.

Our life upon the earth is quite worthless. The more you desire to be spiritual, the more bitter this present life becomes, because it is better understood and the defects of human corruption are easily seen. For to eat, to drink, to watch, to sleep, to rest, to labor, and to be subject to the other necessities of nature can truly be a great misery and affliction to a devout disciple who desires to be released and free from all sin.

3. The disciple who is focused inward is heavily burdened with the necessities of the body in this world. Therefore the prophet devoutly prays to be freed from them, saying, "Deliver me from my necessities, O Lord (Ps 25:17)."

But woe to those who do not know their own misery. And yet a greater woe awaits those who love this miserable and corruptible life. For some cling to it to such a degree (even though by laboring or begging they seldom procure what is needed for subsistence), that even if they would live here forever, they would care nothing for the Kingdom of God.

4. The foolish and faithless of heart are buried deep in worldly things, so much so that they relish nothing except the things of the flesh! Miserable ones! Sadly, they too will find out at the end how vile and worthless were those things which they loved.

The saints of God and Christ's loyal friends see the comforts which pleased the flesh, or those which flourished in this life, as worthless. Their whole hope and affection aspired to eternal possessions. Their whole desire was borne upwards to everlasting and invisible rewards, for fear that they should be drawn downward by the love of visible things.

5. Do not lose your loyal desire to progress in spiritual goods. There is yet time, the hour is not past. Why will you put off your resolution? Arise, begin this very moment, and say, "Now is the time for doing, now is the time to fight, now is the proper time to amend my life." When you are uneasy and troubled, that is the time when you are nearest to receiving a blessing.

You must go through fire and water so that God may bring you into a wealthy place (Ps 66:12). Unless you correct yourself with discipline, you will not conquer your faults. So long as we carry about with us this frail body, we cannot be without sin, we cannot live without weariness and trouble. We would gladly have rest from all misery; but because we have lost innocence through sin, we have also lost true happiness. Therefore we must be patient and wait for the mercy of God, until this tyranny passes, and this mortality is swallowed up (2 Cor 5:4).

6. O how great is the frailty of mortals, which are always prone to evil! Today you confess your sins, and tomorrow you commit again the same sins you just confessed. Now you resolve to avoid a fault, and within an hour you behave as if you had never resolved upon it at all. Therefore we have good cause to humble ourselves, and never to think too highly of ourselves, seeing that we are so frail and unstable. And we may just as quickly be lost by our own negligence, which by much effort and difficulty was attained through grace (Eph 4:7-9).

7. What will become of us in the end, if at the beginning we are lukewarm and idle? Woe unto us, if we choose to rest, as though it

were a time of peace and security, while as yet no sign appears in our life of true holiness (1 Thes 5:3).

Yet perhaps we might begin anew, like good novices, to be instructed on good living, if happily there might be some hope of future change and greater spiritual progress.

❦ 26 ❦

A MEDITATION UPON DEATH

Chapter 23 Focus: Thomas a'Kempis lived to be ninety years old in an age when the average man or woman lived to be forty or fifty (once you lived past childhood). Thus, he lived twice as long as everyone else. He lived by his own maxims and followed the teachings you see in these books and his other writings.

Thomas does not morbidly live in fear of death. Rather, he tells us to prepare for death's inevitability. In Thomas' world, reeling from the aftermath of the Black Plague, famine, and frequent regional wars, he gives an in-depth view of death. In his day, death was close up and frequent. Death was a regular visitor to families: coming uninvited, randomly and suddenly, especially on the young and the frail.

Thomas counsels us to be ready for death by seeking out a life of sanctity now and not being surprised at its sudden arrival. He warns us about being caught with the burden of bitter regrets: regretting the lost opportunities of what we should have done or facing death suddenly without having enough time amend our lives or make corrections.

He exhorts us to model our lives upon the saints, and to make them friends, to lay up treasures in heaven through good works, and to pray earnestly to Christ with lamentations (Mt 6:19-21).

Thomas' perspective was unchanged over his long life. As he survived his family and friends over the years, I imagine that he added more meditations about prayer and pursuit of sanctity. May we all imitate him in this way.

Question: How are you preparing for death?

Chapter 23, In Short.

1. Order your life as if you were to die today.
2. What does it matter if you live a long life, if you change your life so little?
3. Always live so that death may never find you unprepared.
4. Strive to behave in life as you would be in approaching death!
5. Do not put off the work of your salvation to sometime in the future.
6. Learn to die to the world, and begin to live with Christ now.
7. It is foolish to think that of living a long life when you are not guaranteed a single day.
8. Who will remember and pray for you after you are dead?
9. Keep yourself as a stranger and a pilgrim upon the earth.

THE TEXT: OF MEDITATIONS ON DEATH

Very quickly there will be an end of you here. Therefore, listen to how it will be with you in another world. Today you are here, and tomorrow you will be seen no more. And being removed from sight, you quickly fade out of the minds of everyone. O the dullness and hardness of your hearts, which think only of the present, and never look to the future. **You ought to order yourself in every deed and thought as if you were to die this day.**

You would not fear death if you had a good conscience. It is better for you to watch against sinning than to escape from death. If today you are not ready, how will you be ready tomorrow? Tomorrow is an uncertain day, and how do you know that you will even have a tomorrow?

2. What does it matter if you live a long life, when you change your life so little? Ah! Long life does not always result in your amendment of it but often only increases guilt. Oh, that we might spend a single day

in this world as it ought to be spent! There are many who count the years since they were converted, and yet oftentimes have little fruit to show of their conversion.

If it is a fearful thing to die, it may yet be a more fearful thing to live long. Happy are you who have the hour of death always before your eyes, and daily prepare yourself to die. If you have ever seen someone die, consider that you also shall pass away by that same road.

3. When it is morning, reflect that you may not see the evening, and in the evening, do not dare to boast about what you will do tomorrow. Always be prepared, and live so that death may never find you unprepared. Many die suddenly and unexpectedly.

For at such an hour as you cannot foresee, the Son of Man will come (Mt 24:44). When that last hour comes, you will begin to think very differently of your whole life's history, and you will mourn bitterly that you have been so negligent and slothful.

4. When you strive to be in life as you would readily be found in death, you will be happy and wise! These are the things which give you great confidence in a happy death: a perfect disdain of the world, a fervent desire to excel in virtue, the love of discipline, the anguish of repentance, readiness to obey, denial of self, and submission to any adversity for the love of Christ.

While you are in health you have many opportunities for good works, but when you are ill I do not know how many good works you will be able to do. Few are made better by illness: just as those who excessively wander abroad seldom become holy.

5. Do not put off the work of your salvation until sometime in the future. Your friends, relatives, and acquaintances will forget you sooner than you think. It is better for you to provide for that now, in this time, and to send some good prayerful effort before you, than to trust to the help of others.

If you are not anxious for yourself now, who do you think will be anxious for you after your death? Time is most precious now. Now is the acceptable time, now is the day of salvation (2 Cor 6:2). If you do not spend this time well - beware! - instead lay up treasure which will benefit you in heaven (Mt 6:20). The hour will come when you will wish for one day, yes, one more hour, to amend your life, and I do not know whether you will obtain that hour or that change.

6. Oh, dearly beloved, if only you would always live in anticipation and expectation of death! Think of what great danger and fear you might free yourself from. Strive now to live in such a way that in the hour of death you may rejoice rather than fear. Learn now to die to the world, so that you will begin to live with Christ. Learn now to condemn all earthly things, and then you may freely follow Christ. Keep your body under discipline by penance, and then will you be able to have a sure confidence.

7. Oh, you fool! Why do you think that you will live long when you are not guaranteed a single day? How many have been deceived, and suddenly have been snatched away from the body! How many times have you heard how one was slain by the sword, another was drowned, another falling from on high broke his neck, another died at the table, another while at play! One died by fire, another by the sword, another by the pestilence, another by a robber. Death comes to all, and the life of men swiftly passes away like a shadow or a puff of smoke (Jas 4:14).

8. Who will remember you after your death? And who will pray for you? Work, work now, oh dearly beloved, work all that you can. For you do not know when you will die, or what shall happen to you after death. While you have time, lay up for yourself undying riches. Think of nothing but of your salvation. Care only for the things of God. Make yourself friends, by venerating the saints of God and walking in their steps, so that when you fail, you may be received into your eternal home (Lk 16:9).

9. Keep yourself as a stranger and a pilgrim upon the earth, to whom the things of the world do not matter (Ex 2:22). Keep your heart free, and lifted up towards God, for here we have no continuing city (Hb 13:14). Direct your daily prayers to Him with crying and tears, so that your spirit may be found worthy to pass happily after death unto its Lord. Amen.

27

THE JUDGMENT AND PUNISHMENT OF SIN

Chapter 24 Focus: A reminder is given that we will all stand before Christ and be accountable for our actions, our inaction, and our indifference. While we may have many explanations and (we believe) extraordinary circumstances, we are ultimately responsible for our sins.

The disciple should work accordingly with that impending judgment in mind. At the Judgment, the standards of the world will not apply, but only those of Christ. By professing the Faith and working out our salvation and serving God, even under austere conditions, the faithful will be rewarded. It is a promise from God, so you can count on it!

Question: When I stand before the Just Judge, what answer will I give for my sins, acts, and omissions that have gone un-repented?

Chapter 24, In Short.
1. Remember that, in the end, you will stand before a just Judge.
2. The patient disciple finds ample occasions to purify the soul.
3. What will the fire devour except your sins?
4. Every vice will have its corresponding punishment.

5. If you are named and despised as a fool for Christ in this world, you will be seen as wise in the next.

6. A pure and good conscience will rejoice more than learned philosophy.

7. All life is vanity, except to love God and to serve Him.

THE TEXT ON THE JUDGMENT AND PUNISHMENT OF SIN

In all that you do, remember your end and how you will stand before a just Judge, from Whom nothing is hidden, Who is not bribed with gifts, nor accepts excuses, but will judge you with righteous judgment.

O most pitiable and foolish sinner, you who are fearful when confronting an angry enemy face-to-face, what answer will you give to Almighty God, Who knows all your misdeeds? Why not provide for yourself against the Day of Judgment? On that day, no one shall be able to be excused or defended by means of another, but each one shall bear their own burden alone.

Now your labors bring forth fruit.

Now your weeping is acceptable.

Now your groaning is heard. Your sorrow is pleasing to God, and cleansing to your soul (Ps 51:8, 19).

2. Even here on earth, the patient disciple finds many occasions to purify the soul. Grieve more for your persecutor's sins when you suffer injuries by his hand than by weeping over your own sins.

As a disciple, you should pray earnestly for those who spitefully use you and forgive them from your heart. Be quick to ask pardon from others. Offer pity more readily than anger. Seek to deny yourself and fully strive to subdue your flesh to the spirit. Better to purify your soul from sin now than to cling to sins from which we must be purged later. We truly deceive ourselves by the disordered love which we bear towards the flesh.

3. What will the fire devour, except your sins? The more you spare yourself and follow the desires of your flesh, the more severe your punishment will be, and the more fuel you are heaping up for burning.

For where you have sinned, there you will face more serious atonement.

There the slothful will be pricked forward with burning goads and the gluttons will be tormented with intolerable hunger and thirst. There the luxurious and the pleasure lovers will be plunged into burning pitch and stinking brimstone. There the envious shall howl in their grief like mad dogs.

4. Every vice will be accorded its own proper punishment. The proud will be filled with utter confusion, and the covetous will be pinched with miserable poverty. An hour's pain in that place will be more bitter than a hundred years here of the most severe penitence. In this present life, there is some respite from pain as well as the enjoyment of the company of friends. But the lost have no quiet and no comfort.

Now is the time to be anxious and sorrowful for your sins, so that on the Day of Judgment you may boldly stand with the blessed. For then will the righteous stand in great boldness before the face of those that have persecuted him and made no account of his deeds (Wis 1:1). For those who now submit in humility to the judgments of others will then stand up to judge them instead. Then the poor and humble will have great confidence, while the proud will be taken with fear on every side.

5. Then those who learned to be a fool and despised for Christ in this world will be seen to be wise. Then all tribulation will patiently be borne by us and delight us, while the mouths of the ungodly shall be stopped. Then shall all the godly rejoice, and every profane mouth shall mourn. Then the afflicted flesh will rejoice more than if it had been always nourished in delights. Then the humble garment will put on beauty, and the precious robe will hide as vile. Then the little poor cottage will be more commended than the gilded palace. Then enduring patience will have more might than all the power of the world. Then simple obedience will be more highly exalted than all worldly wisdom.

6. Then a pure and good conscience will rejoice more than learned philosophy. Then contempt of riches will have more weight than all the treasure of the children of this world. Then you shall find more

comfort in having prayed devoutly than in having dined sumptuously. Then you will rejoice in having kept silence rather than in having made long speeches. Then holy deeds shall be far stronger than many fine words. Then a strict life and sincere penitence shall bring deeper pleasure than all earthly delights.

Learn now to suffer a little, so that you may be able to escape heavier sufferings then. Prove first here, what you are able to endure hereafter. If now you are able to bear so little, how will you be able to endure eternal torments? If now a little suffering makes you so impatient, what shall hell-fire do to you then? Behold, surely you are not able to have two Paradises, to take your fill or delight here in this world, and to reign with Christ hereafter.

7. If you had ever lived in honors and pleasures even to this day, what would the whole thing profit you if now death came to you in an instant (Mk 8:36)? All, therefore, is vanity, save to love God and to serve only Him (Eccl 1:2).

The disciple who loves God with all his heart does not fear death, nor punishment, nor judgment, nor hell, because perfect love gives sure access to God. But for those who still delight in sin, it is no surprise that such a sinner is afraid of death and judgment. Nevertheless, it is a good thing, if love cannot as yet restrain you from evil, that at least the fear of hell should hold you back. But whoever puts aside the fear of God cannot continue in good for long, but will quickly fall into the snares of the devil.

❧ 28 ❦

THE ZEALOUS AMENDMENT OF OUR WHOLE LIFE.

Chapter 25 Focus: Thomas closes this book by emphasizing that the path to intimacy with God is in the direction of self-denial and ardently pursuing God's will. The pursuit and recognition of this path is as important as the destination itself.

In the second paragraph, Thomas talks about "a certain disciple." It is my opinion that he is once again talking about himself here. His prayer to God is one of a desperate quest for holiness. And our Lord's answer does not disappoint him. We should imitate Thomas' request.

Thomas asks a question as to why the disciple started out on this path. He emphasizes that, through zealous efforts, those vows will be fulfilled. There is clarity of heart and mind in the cultivation of good virtue and fleeing temptation and worldly goods. There is value in being aware of our faults and working on replacing these faults with good habits. In keeping our final destiny in mind, even our own death, we are brought a perspective that requires us to act now on conforming ourselves to God's will.

The disciple, now fully aware of his faults and now free of the world's clutches, is now ready for another conversion, an interior conversion - which Thomas will explore in the next book. I've included Book II, Chapter 1, at the end of this book, to open the door to this inward journey.

Question: Should I continue to pursue holiness? How long?
Chapter 25, In Short.

1. Be watchful and diligent in God's service.

2. Study to find the will of God for the perfection of your good works.

3. Hope in the Lord and do good.

4. Two things are helpful to improve in holiness:
withdrawal from sin and earnest zeal for virtues we are missing.

5. Wherever you see or hear good examples, follow them.

6. Remember your duties, and always remember the Crucified Lord.

7. The serious disciple receives and bears all burdens well.

8. Imagine if we had no other duty than to praise the Lord our God!

9. A disciple begins to enjoy God and be content at the point when she no longer seeks comfort from other creatures.

10. Always remember your end, and how that time lost does not return.

THE TEXT: OF THE ZEALOUS AMENDMENT OF OUR WHOLE LIFE.

Be watchful and diligent in God's service, and think often of why you have renounced the world. Wasn't it so that you might live for God and become a spiritual disciple? Therefore be zealous in your spiritual progress, for soon you will receive the reward for your efforts, and neither fear nor sorrow will come into your borders any more. Now you will labor a little, and find great rest, even everlasting joy. If you remain faithful and zealous in labor, there is no doubt that God will be faithful and bountiful in rewarding you. It is your duty to maintain a good hope that you will attain the victory. However, you must not be too secure for fear that you may become slothful or presumptuous.

2. There was a certain disciple who was anxious of mind: this disciple continually wavered between hope and fear, and on a certain

day felt overwhelmed with grief, and cast himself down in prayer before the altar in church, and meditated within himself, saying, "Oh! If I only knew whether I should still persevere in my pursuit of holiness!"

The disciple then heard a voice within from God say: "And if you did know whether you should persevere in your pursuit of holiness, what would you do?

"Therefore, do now what you would do then, and you shall be assured."

Immediately being comforted and strengthened, the disciple committed to doing God's will, and his perturbation of spirit ceased. The disciple no longer considered curiously searching to know what fate would befall him afterward, but rather studied to inquire what was the good and acceptable will of God for the beginning and perfecting of every good work.

3. "Hope in the Lord and do good," says the Prophet "live well in the land and live secure in its riches (Ps 37:3)." One thing which holds back many from progress and fervent amendment of our lives: the dread of difficulty, or the labor of the conflict.

Nevertheless, those who advance in virtue above all others are those who courageously strive to conquer those disturbing and contrary challenges. For in these obstacles a disciple profits the most and merits greater grace through self-mortification and through an overcomer's spirit.

4. Not all disciples have the same passions to conquer and to mortify, yet whoever is diligent and zealous in this effort attains more progress. While some have stronger passions than others, those who are more temperate in self-discipline but less fervent in the pursuit of virtue will progress more slowly.

Two things are especially helpful to improve in holiness, namely firmness to withdraw ourselves from the sin which by nature we are most inclined, and earnest zeal for that good virtue in which we are most lacking. Strive earnestly to guard against and subdue those faults in yourself which displease you most frequently in others.

5. Gather some benefit to your soul wherever you are, and wherever you see or hear good examples, prompt yourself to follow them. But

where you see anything which is blameworthy, pay attention that you do not participate in the same act; or if at any time you have participated, strive quickly to correct yourself.

As your eye observes others, likewise the eyes of others are upon you. How sweet and pleasant is it to see zealous and godly disciples who are temperate and of good discipline. It is sad and painful to see them walking in a disorderly manner, not practicing the duties to which they are called. It is a hurtful thing to neglect the purpose of their calling and turn their focus upon things which are none of their business.

6. Be mindful of the duties which you have undertaken, and always set before you the remembrance of the Crucified Lord. You ought to be truly repentant as you look upon the life of Jesus Christ. You still have not tried to conform yourself more to Him, even though you have been in the service of God for a long time. A disciple who conducts serious and devout spiritual exercises in the subject of Christ's most holy life and passion will find in that all things profitable and necessary are in abundance. Therefore, there is no need then to seek anything better beyond Jesus.

Oh! If Jesus crucified would come into our hearts, how quickly, and completely would we learn all that we need to know!

7. The serious disciple receives and bears well all burdens laid upon him. Because of a lack of inward consolation, those who are careless and lukewarm have trouble upon trouble and suffer anguish upon every side. Such a disciple is forbidden to seek that which is outward. Those who are living without discipline are exposed to severe ruin. Those who seek easier and lighter discipline will always be in distress because one thing or another will result in their displeasure.

8. Oh! if no other duty lay upon us but to praise the Lord our God with our whole heart and whole voice!

Oh! if you never had the need to eat or drink, or sleep, but were always able to praise God and to give yourself to spiritual exercises alone; then you would be far happier than now, when you must serve the flesh for so many necessities.

Oh! That these necessities were not present, but only the spiritual refreshments of the soul, which alas we taste too seldom.

9. When a disciple has come to this point, not seeking comfort from any creature, it is then that one perfectly begins to enjoy God. It is then that the disciple becomes contented with whatever happens.

Then the disciple will neither rejoice nor be sorrowful for little, but be committed altogether and with full trust in God, Who is all in all to the believer to Whom nothing perishes nor dies, but all things live for Him and obey His every word without delay.

10. Always remember your end, and how that time lost does not return. Without care and diligence, you will never obtain virtue. If you begin to grow cold, things will begin to go ill with you, but if you give yourself over to a zealous nature, you will find great peace and will find your labor lighter because of the grace of God and the love of virtue.

Such a zealous and diligent disciple is ready for all things. It is more difficult to resist your sins and passions than to toil in bodily work. Whoever does not shun small faults falls, little by little, and falls into much greater fault (Sir 19:1). At your day's end, you will be glad that you spent the days profitably.

Watch over yourself, stir yourself up, admonish yourself. And no matter how it goes with others, do not neglect yourself. The more discipline you subscribe to for yourself, the more progress you will make.

Amen.

❧ 29 ☙

BOOK II: ADMONITIONS CONCERNING INTERIOR THINGS.

ON THE INWARD LIFE. "I AM THE TRUTH."
JOHN 14:6.

Chapter Focus: Thomas spends a great deal of time in each of his books telling us what the inward life requires. Having shed the trappings of exterior things back in the Book I, he begins that inward journey here.

This book on Interior Things opens with a discussion about the struggles we face which are even more difficult: those of the inward life and the spiritual interplay of ideas, conscience and closeness to Who our Lord is with respect to ourselves. Our intimacy with God grows in direct proportion to the shedding of the vanities of this world, developing an ardent prayer life, and repositioning our focus from temporal things to the eternal things.

Thomas and Christ, Zwolle, NL

This meditation affected me significantly last spring while attending Mass. The notion of pursuing the interior life overcame me by facing my own lack of growth in this part of my journey. A persistent feeling of laziness had crept into my prayers and worship: I didn't feel like actively praying or looking inward. Rather than look in those dark and dusty places, I wanted to look at the inward side of my eyelids! Like a sloth, I moved imperceptibly slow along God's branches, spiritually napping at every leaf.

Instead of looking for the Kingdom of God, instead of preparing a place for Christ within me, I placed my selfish comfort above pursuing intimacy with God. Instead of looking for the Lord to show up, I looked around to see which of my friends were showing up, giving those that did an approving nod. Instead of contemplating the suffering of Christ, I readied myself to complain to the first person willing to hear about my discomforts of that day.

Breaking out of my self-imposed comfort exile, I turned my thoughts and attentions toward Him, dropping from the secluded, comfortable nest to look for Him. Then the Lord said: "When He reached the place, Jesus looked up and said to him, 'Zacchaeus, come down quickly, for today I must stay at your house.' And [Zacchaeus] came down quickly and received Him with joy (Lk 19:5-6)."

May you encounter the joy of Zacchaeus as you work through Book II of The Imitation of Christ.

Question: Are you following an inward path toward the Kingdom?

Chapter 1, In Short.

1. The Kingdom of God is within you.
2. Prepare a place for Christ.
3. Let God be your love and your [healthy] fear.
4. Heaven is your home.
5. Christ's friends face adversity.
6. The love of Jesus makes you want to review your own life.
7. The truly wise are those who know the true reality of things.
8. If you have a purified, right centered spirit, all things work together for your good.

THE TEXT ON THE INWARD LIFE: "I AM THE TRUTH."
JOHN 14:6

"The kingdom of God is within you," says the Lord.

Luke 17:21

Turn with all your heart to the Lord and forsake this tragic world, and you shall find rest for your soul. Learn to despise outward things and to give yourself to inward movements, and you shall see the kingdom of God come within you. For the kingdom of God is peace and joy in the Holy Spirit, and this Kingdom is not given to the wicked. **Christ will come to you, and show you His consolation if you prepare a worthy mansion for Him within you.** All His glory and beauty is from within, and it pleases Him to dwell there. He often visits the inward soul and holds sweet discussions with them, giving soothing consolation, abundant peace, and wonderful friendships.

2. Go then, faithful soul, prepare your heart for the Bridegroom that He may safely to come to you and dwell within you, for He says so, "If you love me and will keep My commandments: My Father will love you, and We will come to you and make our abode with you (Jn 14:23)." Therefore, prepare a place for Christ and refuse entrance to all others. When you have Christ, you are rich - you have fulfillment. Christ shall be your provider and faithful watchman in all things, so that you will have no need to trust in others, for they will soon change and swiftly pass away, but Christ remains forever and stands by us firmly, even to the end.

3. You should not place your trust in your frail mortal followers, even though they may be useful and dear to our community (Ps 146:2-3). If sometimes you oppose and contradict our community, the sorrow of this burden should not be born by them. People often change direction like the wind. Those who are on your side today may be against you tomorrow. Therefore, put your whole trust in God and let Him be your love and your fear. He will answer for you Himself, and will do for you what is best (Jr 17:7). There is no continuing city for you here (Heb 13:14). You are a stranger and a pilgrim wherever you are, and you shall not have rest unless you are closely united to Christ (Ex 2:22).

4. Why do you cast your eyes here and there, since this is not the place of your rest? Heaven should be your home: all earthly things should be looked upon as if these were simply passing by. All things

pass away and you with them. Look that you do not cleave to these things or else you will be taken with them and perish. Let the Most High God be your contemplation. Let your ceaseless supplications be directed to Christ. If you cannot imagine high and heavenly things, rest in the passion of Christ and dwell constantly in His sacred wounds. For if you devoutly direct your attention to the wounds of Jesus, and the precious marks of the nails and the spear, you shall find great comfort in times of trouble. In this meditation the slights of others will not trouble you, and you will easily be able to bear their unkind words.

5. When Christ was in the world, He was despised and rejected. During His greatest need He was abandoned by His acquaintance and friends to bear these rejections alone. Christ willingly suffered and was despised: do you dare to complain of anything? Christ had many adversaries and detractors: do you wish to have everyone as your friends and benefactors?

When will your patience receive its crown if you never encounter any reproaches? How will you be Christ's friend if you are unwilling to face any adversity? Therefore, sustain yourself with Christ and for Christ if you will reign with Christ.

6. If you had only once entered into the mind and heart of Jesus and tasted even a little of His fiery love, then your own comfort would mean nothing to you. Rather, you would rejoice at the troubles brought upon you. The love of Jesus makes you review your own life and easily see its defects. A lover of Jesus and of truth and an internally focused disciple, free from inordinate affections, can freely turn to God and in spirit be elevated above the self and rest in fruitful peace and enjoyment.

7. Those who know things as they really are and not as they are stated to be or seem to be, are truly wise. They are taught by God more than by men. Those who know how to walk interiorly, and to set little value upon outward things, do not require places nor must they wait for seasons. Rather, they wait – anticipating communion with God.

The disciple who reflects inwardly quickly recollects because that disciple is never given over completely to outward things. No outward efforts or unnecessary occupations stand in their way, but as events play out, so do they fit to the event. Those who are rightly disposed and ordered within care nothing for the strange and perverse conduct of others. They are hindered and distracted in so far as they are moved by outward things.

8. If you had a right spirit within you, and you were purified from evil, all things would work together for your good and profit (Rm 8:28). Because of this, many things displease you and often trouble you: you are not yet perfectly dead to yourself. You are not yet separated from all earthly things. Nothing so defiles and entangles your heart as impure love towards created things. If you reject outward comfort you will be able to contemplate heavenly things and frequently experience inward joy (Jas 1:2).

ABOUT THE AUTHOR

CLOSINGS

Thank you for reading and praying along with me. May we grow close to Christ as we pick up our Cross and follow Him.

We are on this journey together. Our call is to know, love and serve the One, True God, Who is Father, Son and Holy Spirit. We do that best by imitating our Lord Jesus Christ in all that we do: **Therefore, be imitators of Christ!**

Timothy E. Moore, Esq.
Feast of Thomas a'Kempis
July 25th, 2017

Tim Moore

If you would like to read the fictional narrative and Chapter one of Book II, or receive audio versions of each chapter, become a patron by going to: Patreon.com/kempiswriter

All proceeds go to printing and distribution and quality cover art work. Any profits go to support the mission of Springfield Right to Life: Springfieldrtl.org.

Timothyedmoore.com
timothyedmoore.com
tim@timothyedmoore.com

APPENDIX

Key Questions
Key Quotes
Prayers

KEY QUESTIONS FROM BOOK I OF THE IMITATION OF CHRIST.

Each chapter identifies one or more **Key Questions** as the takeaway of the chapter. In every chapter, there could have been more questions for reflections than listed, but this was limited to give you a reflective moment. Further, I did not want this to be a "study guide" or for such devices to overtake the spirit and the power which is inherent in the text of **_The Imitation_**. If you identify a question you think should be added for discussion, I encourage you to share those with me by email: tim@timothyedmoore.com.

1: The Imitation of Christ, and of Contempt of the World and all its Vanities.
   What part of the Life of Christ will I meditate upon?
2: Having a Humble Opinion of Yourself.
   What does my life look like from God's perspective?
   How am I using my knowledge and skills for God's Kingdom?
3: The Knowledge of Truth.
   How do I practice the truths of the Faith in my life?
4: Applying Prudence in What We Do.

KEY QUESTIONS FROM BOOK I OF THE IMITATION OF CHRIST.

How am I prudent in my speech and actions?
5: Reading the Holy Scriptures.
How does God speak to me in Scripture?
6: Inordinate Affections.
What things or pleasures have an unhealthy influence over my interior peace?
7: Avoiding Vain Hope and Pride.
Do I glory in my position in life and count myself as "better" than others?
8: The Dangers of Familiarity.
When have I been overly familiar to the point of committing sin?
What situations cause me these temptations?
9: Obedience and Subjection.
How can I practice obedience of mind, heart, and action?
10: Avoiding a Superfluity of Words.
How can I talk more with God? How can I make my speech with others more meaningful and edifying?
11: Acquiring Peace and Zeal for Spiritual Progress.
What one vice can I root out this year?
12: The Utility of Adversity.
What adversity am I faced with and how is this helping me grow in my faith?
13: On Resisting Temptations.
What are my temptations and how can I ask God to help me overcome these and profit spiritually?
14: Avoiding Rash Judgment.
What measures can I put in place to avoid judging others?
15: Works of Charity.
Does my faith show through my good works?
16: Bearing the Faults of Others.
How can I bear with the faults of others?
17: The Consecrated Life.
Have I consecrated my life to God? What evidence do I have of this consecration?
18: The Example of the Holy Fathers.

Who are the models of faith for you?
19: The Spiritual Exercise of the Devout Disciple.
How can I strengthen my spiritual muscles?
20: The Love of Solitude and Silence.
Do I set aside time for quiet prayer?
21: On Compunction of Heart.
How do I show sorrow and repent for my sins?
How has this sorrow brought me closer to God?
22: Contemplation of the Miseries and Sorrows of This Life.
What material things do I really need?
Do my possessions interfere with my relationship with God?
23: A Meditation Upon Death.
How are you preparing for death?
24: The Judgment and Punishment of Sin.
When I stand before the Just Judge, what answer will I give for my sins, acts, and omissions that have gone un-repented?
25: Of the Zealous Amendment of Our Whole Life.
Should I continue to pursue holiness? How long?

KEY QUOTES

Each chapter identified a "**Key Quote**" which was in bold-face type. This was the quote identified as having the heart of the chapter. In some chapters, this was a difficult task since there were many worthy quotes. You may have your own, of course, and I encourage you to share those with me via email: tim@timothyedmoore.com.

1: The Imitation of Christ, and of Contempt of the World and all its Vanities.

Let it be our most earnest study, therefore, to dwell upon the life of Jesus Christ.

2: Having a Humble Opinion of Yourself.

The highest and most valuable lesson we can learn is this: To truly know and discount ourselves.

3: The Knowledge of Truth.

For certainly, on the Day of Judgment, it will be demanded of us, not what we have read but what we have done; not how well we have spoken, but whether we lived a holy life.

4: Applying Prudence in What We Do.

Alas! we are so weak! We often readily believe and speak evil of others rather than good.

5: Reading the Holy Scriptures.

KEY QUOTES

Seek the Truth in Holy Scripture, not in eloquence.

6: Inordinate Affections.

For true peace of the heart is to be found in resisting your passions, not in yielding to them.

7: Avoiding Vain Hope and Pride.

Do not count yourself better than others, since you will then be accounted worse in the sight of God, who knows what is in your heart.

8: The Dangers of Familiarity.

Associate yourself with the humble and the simple, with the devout and the virtuous and occupy yourself with those things which build up one another.

9: Obedience and Subjection.

Who among us is so wise as to be able to know all things?

10: Avoiding a Superfluity of Words.

The neglect of our spiritual advancement, along with our bad habits, is a great cause of our keeping so little watch upon our mouth.

11: Acquiring Peace and Zeal for Spiritual Progress.

If every year we rooted out one vice, we would soon become perfect.

12: The Utility of Adversity.

When a disciple of good will is troubled, or tempted, or afflicted with evil thoughts, then it is easier to understand the need for God, without Whom you can do no good.

13: On Resisting Temptations.

No one is so perfect and holy as not to have some temptations, and we never can be wholly free from them.

14: Avoiding Rash Judgment.

If God were always the sole object of our desire, we would be less troubled by the erring judgment of our fancy.

15: Works of Charity.

Whoever does much, loves much.

16: Bearing the Faults of Others.

If you cannot make your own self what you desire, how can you correct another to your own liking?

17: The Consecrated Life.

If you are to lead a Christ-centered life, you will have to be counted as a fool for Christ.

18: The Example of the Holy Fathers.

Would to God that advancement in virtue was not completely asleep in those of you who have so often seen so many examples of the devout!

19: The Spiritual Exercise of the Devout Disciple.

For man proposes, but God disposes.

20: The Love of Solitude and Silence.

Leave vain things to vain people, and mind the things which God has commanded you.

21: On Compunction of Heart.

If you thought more about your impending death rather than how long your life will be, you would eagerly strive to improve your life.

22: Contemplation of the Miseries and Sorrows of This Life.

When you are uneasy and troubled, that is the time when you are nearest to receiving a blessing.

23: A Meditation Upon Death.

You ought to order yourself in every deed and thought as if you were to die this day.

24: The Judgment and Punishment of Sin.

The disciple who loves God with all his heart does not fear death, nor punishment, nor judgment, nor hell, because perfect love gives sure access to God.

25: Of the Zealous Amendment of Our Whole Life.

"And if you did know whether you should persevere in your pursuit of holiness, what would you do?

"Therefore, do now what thou would do then, and you shall be assured."

PRAYERS

The Imitation of Christ contains many prayers. However, in Book One, there are only a few. Those are listed here by chapter and paragraph numbers. In future volumes, you will see many, many more. Accordingly, listed for your meditation and reflection, are a series of prayers typical of the daily devotional life.
   From Chapter 3: The Knowledge of Truth.

O God, You who are the Truth, make me one with You in everlasting love.
It often wearies me to read and listen to many things.
All that I wish for and desire is in You.
Let all the doctors hold their peace;
Let all creation keep silence before You.
Speak alone to me, Lord. Amen.

From Chapter 19: The Spiritual Exercise of the Devout Disciple.

"Help me, O God, in my good resolutions,
and in Your holy service,

and grant that this day I may make a good beginning,
for prior to this I have done nothing!"

From a Collection of Catholic Prayers:
1. The Lord's Prayer, The "Our Father."
Or Father, Who art in heaven,
Hallowed be Thy Name.
Thy Kingdom come.
Thy Will be done, on earth as it is in Heaven.
Give us this day our daily bread.
And forgive us our trespasses,
as we forgive those who trespass against us.
And lead us not into temptation,
but deliver us from evil. Amen.

2. The Hail Mary.
Hail Mary,
Full of Grace,
The Lord is with Thee.
Blessed art thou among Women,
and blessed is the fruit of Thy womb, Jesus.
Holy Mary, Mother of God, pray for us sinners
now, and at the hour of death. Amen.

3. The Morning Offering.
O Jesus, through the Immaculate Heart of Mary, I offer you my prayers, works, joys and sufferings of this day.

In union with the whole Church, and the Holy Sacrifice of the Mass throughout the world.

In reparation for my sins, and those of my associates. For the intentions of all my relatives and friends, and in particular for the intentions of the Holy Father this day.

Amen.

4. Come, Holy Spirit.

Come, Holy Spirit, fill the hearts of Thy faithful: and enkindle in them the fire of Thy love.

V. Send forth Thy Spirit and they shall be created.

R. And Thou shalt renew the face of the earth.

Let us pray. O God, Who instructs the hearts of the faithful by the light of the Holy Spirit,

grant us in the same Spirit to be truly wise, and ever to rejoice in His consolation.

Through Christ our Lord. Amen.

Latin:

Veni, Sancte Spiritus, reple tuorum corda fidelium: et tui amoris in eis ignem accende.

V. Emitte Spiritum tuum, et creabuntur.

R. Et renovabis faciem terrae.

Oremus. Deus, qui corda fidelium Sancti Spiritus illustratione docuisti:

Da nobis in eodem Spiritu recta sapere; et de eius semper consolatione gaudere.

Per Christum Dominum nostrum. Amen.

5. The Act of Contrition.

O my God, I am heartily sorry for having offended You, and I detest all my sins, because I dread the loss of heaven, and the pains of hell;

but most of all because they offend You, my God, Who are all good and deserving of all my love.

I firmly resolve, with the help of Thy grace, to confess my sins, to do penance,

and to amend my life. Amen.

PRAYERS

6. Anima Christi.
   Soul of Christ, sanctify me.
   Body of Christ, save me.
   Blood of Christ, inebriate me.
   Water from the side of Christ's, wash me.
   Passion of Christ, strengthen me.
   O good Jesus, hear me.
   Within Your wounds hide me.
   Separated from You, let me never be.
   From the malicious enemy defend me.
   In the hour of my death call me.
   And bid me come unto Thee.
   That I may praise You forever with Your Angels
   and with Your Saints. Amen.

7. The Memorare.

Remember, O most gracious Virgin Mary, that never was it known that anyone who fled to Your protection, implored Your help, or sought Your intercession was left unaided.

Inspired by this confidence, I fly unto You, O Virgin of virgins, my Mother;

to You do I come, before You I stand, sinful and sorrowful.

O Mother of the Word Incarnate, despise not my petitions,

but in Your mercy hear and answer me. Amen.

8. Hail, Holy Queen.
   Hail, Holy Queen, Mother of Mercy!
   Our Life, our Sweetness, and our Hope!

To You do we cry, poor banished children of Eve. To You do we send up our sighs, mourning and weeping in this valley of tears.

Turn, then, O most gracious advocate, thine eyes of mercy toward us, and after this, our exile, show unto us, the blessed fruit of Thy womb, Jesus.

O clement, O loving, O sweet Virgin Mary,..

O Mother of the Word Incarnate, despise not my petition, but in Your mercy,

Hear and answer me. Amen.

9. Prayer to St. Michael.

St. Michael the Archangel, defend us in battle.
Be our defense against the wickedness and snares of the Devil.
May God rebuke him, we humbly pray,
and do Thou, O Prince of the heavenly hosts,
by the power of God, thrust into hell Satan,
and all the evil spirits, who prowl about the world
seeking the ruin of souls. Amen.

10. Prayer Before The Crucifix.

Look down upon me, good and gentle Jesus, while before Your face I humbly kneel and,

with burning soul, pray and beseech You to fix deep in my heart lively sentiments of faith, hope and charity; true contrition for my sins, and a firm purpose of amendment.

While I contemplate, with great love and tender pity, Your five most precious wounds,

pondering over them within me and calling to mind the words which David, Your prophet, said of You, my Jesus: "They have pierced My hands and My feet, they have numbered all My bones."

Amen.

11. The Apostles' Creed.

I believe in God, the Father Almighty, Creator of Heaven and earth; and in Jesus Christ,

His only Son Our Lord, Who was conceived by the Holy Spirit, born of the Virgin Mary,
    suffered under Pontius Pilate, was crucified, died, and was buried.
    He descended into Hell; the third day He rose again from the dead;
    He ascended into Heaven, and sits at the right hand of God, the Father almighty -
    from thence He shall come to judge the living and the dead.
    I believe in the Holy Spirit, the holy Catholic Church, the communion of saints,
    the forgiveness of sins, the resurrection of the body and life everlasting. Amen.

12. The Glory Be.

    Glory be to the Father,
    and to the Son,
    and to the Holy Spirit.
    As it was in the beginning,
    is now, and ever shall be,
    world without end. Amen.

13. The Litany of Humility.

    O Jesus! Meek and humble of heart, Hear me.
    From the desire of being esteemed,
    Deliver me, Jesus.
    From the desire of being loved...
    From the desire of being extolled ...
    From the desire of being honored ...
    From the desire of being praised ...
    From the desire of being preferred to others...
    From the desire of being consulted ...
    From the desire of being approved ...
    From the fear of being humiliated ...
    From the fear of being despised...
    From the fear of suffering rebukes ...

From the fear of being calumniated ...
From the fear of being forgotten ...
From the fear of being ridiculed ...
From the fear of being wronged ...
From the fear of being suspected ...
That others may be loved more than I,
Jesus, grant me the grace to desire it.
That others may be esteemed more than I ...
That, in the opinion of the world,
others may increase and I may decrease ...
That others may be chosen and I set aside ...
That others may be praised and I go unnoticed
That others may be preferred to me in everything...
That others may become holier than I,
provided that I may become as holy as I should...

14. The Magnificat (The Prayer Of Mary (Lk 1:46-55)).

My soul proclaims the greatness of the Lord!
My spirit rejoices in God my Savior! For He has looked with favor on His lowly servant.
From this day all generations will call me blessed:
the Almighty has done great things for me, and holy is His Name.
He has mercy on those who fear Him in every generation.
He has shown the strength of His Arm,
He has scattered the proud in their conceit.
He has cast down the mighty from their thrones, and has lifted up the lowly.
He has filled the hungry with good things, and the rich He has sent away empty.
He has come to the help of his servant Israel for
He remembered His promise of mercy, the promise
He made to our fathers,
to Abraham and his children forever.

PRAYERS

Latin:

Magnificat anima mea Dominum;
Et exultavit spiritus meus in Deo salutari meo,
Quia respexit humilitatem ancillae suae; ecce enim ex hoc beatam me dicent omnes generationes.
Quia fecit mihi magna qui potens est, et sanctum nomen ejus,
Et misericordia ejus a progenie in progenies timentibus eum.
Fecit potentiam brachio suo;
Dispersit superbos mente cordis sui.
Deposuit potentes de sede, et exaltavit humiles.
Esurientes implevit bonis, et divites dimisit inanes.
Sucepit Israel, puerum suum, recordatus misericordiae suae,
Sicut locutus est ad patres nostros, Abraham et semeni ejus in saecula.

15. Prayer for Those with Profound Disabilities.

Lord Jesus Christ, You know the pain of brokenness,

You took our weaknesses upon Your shoulders and bore it to the wood of the cross.

Hear our prayers for our brothers and sisters whose bodies fail them and whose minds are crippled by the ravages of disease.

Implant a love for them deep within our hearts that we, disfigured and disabled by our sin, may treasure and nurture the gifts of their lives.

May we find You in their weakness, and console You in our care for them.

For You are Lord, forever and ever.

Amen.

16. Prayer for Those Close to Death

Lord Jesus Christ,

As You stood by the bed of good Saint Joseph and gently led him home to heaven, so shepherd every soul about to die to a paradise of perfect peace.

Let the tears we shed upon their passing stand witness to our love for them and the

depth of our thanksgiving for the gift of their lives and the grace of a good death.

For You are Lord, forever and ever. Amen.

Copyright © 2017 by Timothy E. Moore, Esq.

All rights reserved.

No part of this book may be reproduced in any form or by any electronic or mechanical means, including information storage and retrieval systems, without written permission from the author, except for the use of brief quotations in a book review.